TRADITIONS OF CHRISTIAN SPIRITUALITY

POVERTY AND JOY

POVERTY AND JOY

The Franciscan Tradition

WILLIAM J. SHORT OFM

SERIES EDITOR:
Philip Sheldrake

ORBIS BOOKS

Maryknoll, New York 10545

The Catholic Foreign Mission Society of America (Maryknoll) recruits and trains people for overseas missionary service. Through Orbis Books, Maryknoll aims to foster the international dialogue that is essential to mission. The books published, however, reflect the opinions of their authors and are not meant to represent the official position of the society. To obtain more information about Maryknoll and Orbis Books, please visit our website at www.maryknoll.org.

First published in 1999 by
Darton, Longman and Todd Ltd.
1 Spencer Court
140–142 Wandsworth High Street
London SW18 4JJ
Great Britain

Published in the USA in 1999 by
Orbis Books
P.O. Box 308
Maryknoll, New York 10545–0308
U.S.A.

Copyright © 1999 by William J. Short
Orbis ISBN 1–57075–295–8

Printed and bound in Great Britain by CPI Bath

Library of Congress Cataloging-in-Publication Data

Short, William J.
    Poverty and joy : the Franciscan tradition / William J. Short.
        p.   cm.—(Traditions of Christian spirituality series)
    Includes bibliographical references and index.
    ISBN 1–57075–295–8 (pbk.)
    1. Franciscans—Spiritual life. 2. Spiritual life—Catholic
Church—History. I. Title. II. Series: Traditions of Christian
spirituality.
    BX3603.S46 1999
    255′.3—dc21   99–24173
                                                               CIP

IOANNI
FRATRI
MAGISTRO

'... amico, è ito tra fiori'
(Giacomo Akira)

CONTENTS

ACKNOWLEDGEMENTS

The Franciscan School of Theology, its President William Cieslak, its faculty, staff and students graciously allowed me the freedom of a sabbatical to complete this task. Paschal Hocum asked questions that helped me to organise my otherwise scattered thoughts, while Michael Guinan kept me alert to new publications, and Joe Chinnici's insights on the evangelical life have served me constantly. Kathleen Moffatt and my brothers and sisters of the Franciscan Federation encouraged me to face the Christ incarnate. My sisters, the Poor Clares of Bordentown, kindly listened to my ideas about Franciscan contemplation, and Claire André patiently followed my progress.

The faculty and students, past and present, of the Doctoral Program in Christian Spirituality at the Graduate Theological Union encouraged me, *verbo et exemplo*, to make this contribution to our common endeavour. Douglas Burton-Christie has my special thanks for suggesting my participation in this series to Philip Sheldrake who kindly reviewed boxes of my notes in preparation for this project.

Wayne Hellmann and Regis Armstrong continue to be my best mentors in the complex world of Franciscan documents. Mel Jurisich assured that I had time, John Hardin looked after my needs, and Josef Prochnow cared for my garden, while Mario DiCicco helped assure funding. Finian McGinn and Steve Barnufsky, Ed Dunn, Richard McManus, Miguel Obregon and Ben Innes demonstrated the support of my Franciscan Province of St Barbara. I hope that two of my earliest teachers in the Franciscan tradition, John Vaughn and Kenan

Osborne, will find in this volume another reason to celebrate their fiftieth anniversary as Franciscans.

Turin
Christmas 1998

PREFACE TO THE SERIES

Nowadays, in the western world, there is a widespread hunger for spirituality in all its forms. This is not confined to traditional religious people let alone to regular churchgoers. The desire for resources to sustain the spiritual quest has led many people to seek wisdom in unfamiliar places. Some have turned to cultures other than their own. The fascination with Native American or Aboriginal Australian spiritualities is a case in point. Other people have been attracted by the religions of India and Tibet or the Jewish Kabbalah and Sufi mysticism. One problem is that, in comparison to other religions, Christianity is not always associated in people's minds with 'spirituality'. The exceptions are a few figures from the past who have achieved almost cult status such as Hildegard of Bingen or Meister Eckhart. This is a great pity for Christianity East and West over two thousand years has given birth to an immense range of spiritual wisdom. Many traditions continue to be active today. Others that were forgotten are being rediscovered and reinterpreted.

It is a long time since an extended series of introductions to Christian spiritual traditions has been available in English. Given the present climate, it is an opportune moment for a new series which will help more people to be aware of the great spiritual riches available within the Christian tradition.

The overall purpose of the series is to make selected spiritual traditions available to a contemporary readership. The books seek to provide accurate and balanced historical and thematic treatments of their subjects. The authors are also conscious of the need to make connections with contemporary experience and values without being artificial or reducing a tradition to one dimension. The authors are well versed in reliable scholarship about the traditions they describe. However, their intention is that the books should be fresh in style and accessible to the general reader.

One problem that such a series inevitably faces is the word 'spirituality'. For example, it is increasingly used beyond religious circles and does not necessarily imply a faith tradition. Again, it could mean substantially different things for a Christian and a Buddhist. Within Christianity itself, the word in its modern sense is relatively recent. The reality that it stands for differs subtly in the different contexts of time and place. Historically, 'spirituality' covers a breadth of human experience and a wide range of values and practices.

No single definition of 'spirituality' has been imposed on the authors in this series. Yet, despite the breadth of the series there is a sense of a common core in the writers themselves and in the traditions they describe. All Christian spiritual traditions have their source in three things. First, while drawing on ordinary experience and even religious insights from elsewhere, Christian spiritualities are rooted in the Scriptures and particularly in the gospels. Second, spiritual traditions are not derived from abstract theory but from attempts to live out gospel values in a positive yet critical` way within specific historical and cultural contexts. Third, the experiences and insights of individuals and groups are not isolated but are related to the wider Christian tradition of beliefs, practices and community life. From a Christian perspective, spirituality is not just concerned with prayer or even with narrowly religious activities. It concerns the whole of human life, viewed in terms of a conscious relationship with God, in Jesus Christ, through the indwelling of the Holy Spirit and within a community of believers.

The series as a whole includes traditions that probably would not have appeared twenty years ago. The authors themselves have been encouraged to challenge, where appropriate, inaccurate assumptions about their particular tradition. While conscious of their own biases, authors have nonetheless sought to correct the imbalances of the past. Previous understandings of what is mainstream or 'orthodox' sometimes need to be questioned. People or practices that became marginal demand to be re-examined. Studies of spirituality in the past frequently underestimated or ignored the role of women. Sometimes the treatments of spiritual traditions were culturally one-sided because they were written from an uncritical western European or North Atlantic perspective.

However, any series is necessarily selective. It cannot hope to do full justice to the extraordinary variety of Christian spiritual traditions. The principles of selection are inevitably open to question. I hope that an appropriate balance has been maintained between a sense of the likely readership on the one hand and the dangers of narrowness on the other. In the end, choices had to be made and the result is inevitably weighted in favour of traditions that have achieved 'classic' status or which seem to capture the contemporary imagination. Within these limits, I trust that the series will offer a reasonably balanced account of what the Christian spiritual tradition has to offer.

As editor of the series I would like to thank all the authors who agreed to contribute and for the stimulating conversations and correspondence that sometimes resulted. I am especially grateful for the high quality of their work which made my task so much easier. Editing such a series is a complex undertaking. I have worked closely throughout with Morag Reeve of Darton, Longman & Todd and Robert Ellsberg of Orbis Books. I am immensely grateful to them for their friendly support and judicious advice. Without them this series would never have come together.

PHILIP SHELDRAKE
Sarum College, Salisbury

ABBREVIATIONS

The following are the standard abbreviations used to refer to the writings of Francis and Clare and other early Franciscan texts.

I. Writings of Saint Francis

Adm	Admonitions
BenLeo	Blessing for Brother Leo
CantSol	Canticle of Brother Sun
CantExh	Canticle of Exhortation
EpAnt	Letter to St Anthony
EpCler	Letter to the Clergy
1EpCust	First Letter to the Custodians
2EpCust	Second Letter to the Custodians
1EpFid	First Version of the Letter to the Faithful
2EpFid	Second Version of the Letter to the Faithful
EpLeo	Letter to Brother Leo
EpMin	Letter to a Minister
EpOrd	Letter to the Entire Order
EpRect	Letter to the Rulers of the Peoples
ExhLd	Exhortation to the Praise of God
ExPat	Prayer Inspired by the Our Father
FormViv	Form of Life for St Clare
LaudDei	Praises of God
LaudHor	Praises To Be Said at All the Hours
OffPass	Office of the Passion
OrCruc	Prayer Before the Crucifix
RegB	Later Rule

RegNb	Earlier Rule
RegEr	Rule for Hermitages
SalBVM	Salutation of the Blessed Virgin Mary
SalVirt	Salutation of the Virtues
Test	Testament
TestSen	Testament Written at Siena
UltVol	Last Will Written for St Clare
VpLaet	Dictate on True and Perfect Joy

II. Writings of Saint Clare

1LAg	First Letter to St Agnes of Prague
2LAg	Second Letter to St Agnes of Prague
3LAg	Third Letter to St Agnes of Prague
4LAg	Fourth Letter to St Agnes of Prague
LEr	Letter to Ermentrude of Bruges
RCl	Rule of St Clare
TestCl	Testament of St Clare
BCl	Blessing of St Clare

III. Other Early Franciscan Sources

1Cel	First Life of St Francis by Thomas of Celano
2Cel	Second Life of St Francis by Thomas of Celano
3Cel	Treatise on the Miracles by Thomas of Celano
AP	Anonymous of Perugia
JdV	Witness of Jacques de Vitry
L3S	Legend of the Three Companions
LegCl	Legend of St Clare
LM	Major Life of St Francis by St Bonaventure
LMin	Minor Life of St Francis by St Bonaventure
LP	Legend of Perugia
Proc	Acts of the Process of Canonisation of St Clare

SC   Sacrum Commercium
SP   Mirror of Perfection

INTRODUCTION

What the Poverello wished to do was to bring again to
[our] notice the science of holy love . . . And in fact, from
the 'bubbling-up well' of his heart there has come a whole
school of spirituality, that has propagated itself down the
centuries as, we consider, the richest of all, incontestably
one of the most beautiful, and one which has most decisively left its stamp on the history of the Church.

In our day it has fallen into unmerited neglect, and it
is in order that it may be once more known and honoured
by the re-editing of the most beautiful works of the Franciscan School that this new collection has been made.[1]

These lines were written some seventy years ago by a Belgian
Franciscan, Martial Lekeux, a former captain in the Belgian
army, who began writing about Franciscan spirituality after
his harrowing experience of World War I. He was writing to
launch a series of books on the Franciscan school of spirituality,
designed to commemorate, in 1926, the seventh centenary of
the death of Francis of Assisi. As I was preparing this volume
on the Franciscan tradition of Christian spirituality, I
stumbled across the story of Lekeux's project, and it struck
me as an appropriate link with my own.

Lekeux's writings on the Franciscan tradition began with
an odd experience. During the war, a priest in the village of
Boitshoucke, near the front, gave the young soldier a small,
battered book, *The Catechism of the Love of God* by a nearly
forgotten Franciscan author, Fulgence Bottens (d. 1717). 'I took
it without enthusiasm,' writes Lekeux, because it seemed to

be only a standard catechism 'drawn up in questions and answers in old Flemish'. But that night and the next day he kept reading it: 'My soul burned within me as had the souls of the disciples at Emmaus.' The young soldier had discovered the Franciscan tradition of spirituality.

Lekeux's experience of personal connection with one author from a tradition of spirituality prompted him to undertake a project: making accessible to a wider public in the early twentieth century the works of major figures from the Franciscan 'school' of spirituality. The present volume seeks to do the same, for a different public at the beginning of the twenty-first century.

WHO ARE THE FRANCISCANS?

The 'Franciscan Movement' or 'Franciscan Family' has included from its very beginnings a rich diversity, and seems to resist even the most earnest attempts to turn it into a 'system'. Even to describe 'Franciscans' today is an imposing project. The Family embraces the laity in their millions, men and women of the Secular Franciscan Order (Brothers and Sisters of Penance, or Third Order). There are hundreds of thousands of men and women in hundreds of religious communities growing out of the Order of Penance (the Third Order Regular). The Poor Clares, sometimes called the Second Order (the 'Poor Sisters' founded by Clare) and the Conceptionist nuns, founded by Beatrice of Silva, live in hundreds of autonomous communities scattered around the globe. And there are tens of thousands of lay and ordained men of the First Order (the Friars Minor or 'Lesser Brothers'), divided into three major branches: Friars Minor Conventual, Friars Minor Capuchin and the Friars Minor, sometimes called Observants, or 'of the Leonine Union' (after Pope Leo XIII). There are Franciscan communities in the Anglican Communion (the Society of Saint Francis) and communities like that of 'Graymoor Franciscans' (the Society of the Atonement), which began as an Anglican community and later became Roman Catholic.

Beginning in the nineteenth century there also arose a so-called 'Fourth Order' of scholars and admirers of Francis, many of whom were responsible for important new discoveries about the Franciscan tradition. Chief among these was Paul Sabatier, of the French Reformed Church, whose *Vie de Saint François*, published in 1893, ignited a lively debate about the figure of Francis, the so-called 'Franciscan Question'. A host of other scholars and popular writers have described individuals and themes of the Franciscan tradition over the course of the last hundred years (not to mention those of the previous seven hundred).

FRANCIS, CLARE AND THE FRANCISCAN TRADITION

To understand Franciscan spirituality requires familiarity with its founding figures, Francis and Clare of Assisi, and with the context in which they lived. In the first chapter their biographical and historical background will be sketched briefly. In addition, the basic structure of their spirituality will be outlined, as a foundation for understanding the later Franciscan tradition. In succeeding chapters some of the important themes from the tradition will be described, using Francis and Clare as points of departure, keeping in mind concerns evident in the contemporary revival of interest in spirituality.[2]

What follows is thus more than a study of the spirituality of Francis and Clare, though they have a privileged place. It is also about the way a tradition came to life. Those who first came into contact with the Franciscan movement after Francis and Clare had died inherited a written and oral tradition inspired by the experience of both. With the passing of time, new participants modulated, enriched and constantly reinterpreted the tradition. To the present day, followers of the Franciscan way have constantly translated the tradition into new languages, cultures and historical contexts, so that it comes to us as we now know it. A comprehensive examination of even the major spiritual writers of the Franciscan school throughout the last eight centuries would go far beyond the bounds of this survey. Such a work is needed, and has already been begun, thanks to the hard work of contemporary Franciscan scholars.[3] My intention is to provide only a sample, a taste or (honouring its Italian origins) an *aperitivo* of this tradition. This modest intention must also serve as some excuse for the inevitable omissions in this volume, of which I am only too conscious.

It is my hope that a better understanding of themes and personalities from the Franciscan tradition can offer the reader some sense of this 'minority party' within the great assembly of Christian spiritual traditions. Chaotic and intuitive, creative and affectionate, radical and obedient, the Franciscan tradition may offer to those searching for a 'path' of spirituality an appealing itinerary.

1. 'TO FOLLOW THE FOOTSTEPS OF OUR LORD JESUS CHRIST'

The word 'new' recurs frequently in the comments of early observers of the Franciscan movement. Francis himself seemed to many in his day a new kind of Christian, one who did not fit easily within the categories of his day. Instead of accepting one of the well-established forms of Christian life available in the early 1200s, he chose the more difficult way, creating a new 'form of life', as he called it, different from the prevailing monastic and canonical forms then in favour. And what drove that desire to create something new was his deep conviction that it was 'the Lord Jesus Christ' himself who was guiding him.[1] Followers soon arrived: 'The Lord gave me brothers,' he said.[2] They formed a fraternity, followed a form of life based on the gospel. In part contemplatives, in part popular preachers, they lived by the work of their hands, frequently with the sick, and begged when they needed to. That early fraternity soon assumed the form of a religious Order (the Order of Lesser Brothers or 'Friars Minor') with a rule, officially approved a few years before Francis' death, and soon included learned members and priests.

Clare of Assisi, despite violent opposition from the men in her family, decided to follow this new way of gospel life, inspired by both the preaching and the example of Francis. She developed the new 'form of life' in a women's community marked by sisterly communion, prayer and manual labour, with no stable sources of revenue. Combining elements of monastic life with the life of lay women penitents she created her own unique expression of 'life according to the Holy Gospel'. Its innovative character, especially Clare's insistence on work and begging to support her sisters, alarmed church authorities, who time and again attempted to convince her to accept a more secure, more traditional lifestyle. Forty years after beginning her 'evangelical experiment', Clare's own Rule was approved, the first of its kind, written for women by a woman.

As Francis reflected upon his life as he was approaching death, he left us in his Testament a remarkable and simple account of how the Franciscan tradition began: 'The Lord inspired me to begin to do penance in this way . . .' He then goes on to recount the stages of his conversion: being turned from revulsion in the presence of lepers to the experience of 'sweetness' when among them; his faith in churches (which he repaired); the coming of his first followers; and the 'form of life' which the Lord inspired him to write 'in few and simple words'.[3]

The great discovery for Francis, and what struck his contemporaries as new, was something as old as the Gospels themselves. The Lord had inspired in him the desire to live the kind of life that Jesus lived with his disciples. This may seem a commonplace to us today. We speak frequently of 'a gospel life', or 'gospel values', and perhaps take the phrase for granted. Not so in Francis' day: religious communities sought to imitate the early Christian community at Jerusalem, described in Acts (2:44–7; 4:32–5). With its orderly rhythm of 'the breaking of bread and the prayers', listening to the teaching of the apostles, and its members sharing their goods in common, this model had served both the ancient communities of monks and the more recent communities of clerics regular as a healthy and moderate norm of discipleship.

Francis was inspired to follow a way of life that was less settled, one that would resemble more closely the life of Jesus himself, shared with Mary and the disciples during the brief years of their mission in Galilee and the surrounding territory. The reference to Jesus, Mary and the disciples is intentional: Francis saw in them the pattern for his own life, and that of his followers. '[The Lord Jesus Christ] was a poor man and a transient and lived on alms, He and the Blessed Virgin and His disciples.'[4]

This life of transients, dependent on the generosity of others while they travel, struck a chord within Francis. In their poverty, Jesus and the members of his 'community' were the best examples of what it means to proclaim the reign of God and live in its presence. Thomas of Celano, one of Francis' followers who first wrote the story of his life, portrays Francis as he heard the Gospel being read on one occasion in the early days of his conversion. The passage about the sending of the disciples moves Francis deeply, and he asks the priest after Mass to explain the text to him (it was evidently read in Latin, which Francis understood, but not well).

In this passage Jesus sends the disciples to preach the reign of God, instructing them to travel without silver or gold, extra tunics, without sandals or walking-sticks.[5] After hearing the priest's explanation of the Gospel, Francis cries out: 'This is what I want, this is what I desire, this is what I long for with all my heart.'[6] Clearly Thomas is trying to communicate, two years after Francis' death, the enthusiasm that led him to summarise his way of life with the words, 'to observe the Holy Gospel of Our Lord Jesus Christ'.[7]

Clare begins her Rule by saying that the 'form of life' of the Poor Sisters (the first name of her community) was inaugurated by Francis himself, and that life is 'to observe the Holy Gospel of Our Lord Jesus Christ'.[8] She considered her life with her sisters a 'mirror' of the gospel, reflecting the face of Christ to the world, particularly to the violent and troubled world of Assisi itself. Clare and her community preached the gospel by their living example of poverty and peaceful unity. After her death, witnesses among her own sisters and the citizens of Assisi testified to this example at the canonisation proceedings that examined her life and virtues. Those suffering from physical and mental illness found comfort and healing in her presence; mercenaries turned away from attacking Assisi after encountering her; she fed the hungry, washed the feet of her sisters, and encouraged other women who were founding communities modelled on hers. And in all this, she constantly returned to the theme of following 'the footsteps of the Lord', like the disciples.

Francis and Clare set out to follow the gospel as their Rule. Was this really new? No, not entirely. Others in the century preceding them had already pointed to the gospel itself as their rule of life. In France, Stephen of Muret (d. 1124) had pointed to the gospel as the norm for his community's common life, rather than the Rule of Benedict or Augustine. Peter Waldo, a converted merchant from Lyons, had patterned his own life on the model of itinerant gospel preaching. His followers, the Poor of Lyons (and later, the Waldensians) along with the Humiliati in Northern Italy, and the Poor Catholics led by Durand of Huesca, had all turned to the descriptions of life in the gospel as their norm for Christian community life.

Then why did Francis and his way of life strike people as new? Perhaps it was because, unlike the other groups mentioned, he managed to stay in close communion with the Papacy, under Innocent III, Honorius III and Gregory IX, avoiding some of the intermittent condemnations suffered by the other groups. Perhaps it was because he combined austerity of life with an infectious joy, service of the poor with lyrical delight in creatures, popular preaching with silent contemplation, and missionary journeys with long periods in mountain hermitages.

Clare's genius lay in providing a form of the gospel life that was accessible to women outside the bounds of traditional monasticism. The life of her community shared some of the features of the lay penitent communities of the Beguines (called *bizzocche* in central Italy). They relied on the work of their hands, notably in textile work, to support themselves, something considered unusual for women of Clare's noble rank. And when they did not receive enough for their labour to provide the necessities of life, they relied on begging, especially that done by Francis' brothers, to supply their needs. Unlike nearby Benedictine monasteries, the Assisi community, located at the little church of San Damiano, did not require that the women provide a dowry for entrance. The large number of women's communities that imitated the life of the sisters of San Damiano during Clare's lifetime testifies to the enormous appeal their way of life exerted within the burgeoning women's religious revival of the thirteenth century.

One last element that would characterise as truly 'new' this evangelical movement of Clare and Francis was the body of Francis himself. News spread quickly after his death that he was marked with the stigmata, the marks of the passion of Christ, in his hands, feet and side. This 'new miracle', as it was hailed at the time of his canonisation, set him apart from earlier saints, making him seem to future generations an icon in flesh and blood, a living image of Christ, one perfectly conformed to the Lord he strove to follow. Perhaps no element contributed more to the popular devotion to Francis as a saint, and no other element created as much controversy about him in later centuries. In fact it was exaggerated emphasis on the 'Conformities' of the life of Christ and that of Francis that would later draw the wrath of Martin Luther in his criticism of 'idolatrous' veneration of saints at the time of the Reformation.

But at this point we need to take a step backward, to begin to fill in the historical context in which Francis, Clare and their followers first developed what would later become the Franciscan, or Francis-Clarian tradition. To do this, we need to understand something of the lived experience of the early members of this movement, especially Francis and Clare themselves. Here we can look at only the highlights of their experience: whole libraries have been written on more complex matters of dates and times, with tomes of critical editions of early Franciscan texts.[9] For our purposes here we will limit ourselves to some essential background information about the life and times of Francis and Clare.

ASSISI

Both Francis and Clare were born into the society of Assisi, in north-central Italy, in the late twelfth century, Francis in 1181 or 1182, Clare in 1193 or 1194. The earlier culture of feudalism was giving way to new forces in those years, particularly in central Italy. The new class of merchants asserted itself; towns like Assisi rivalled feudal manors in political importance; coined money and trade replaced barter and subsistence agriculture as the driving forces in the economy. Improved and safer roads, so necessary for travelling businessmen, opened places like Assisi to the possibility of travel throughout Italy, beyond the Alps into France and the rest of Europe, and, by sea route, to the Middle East and North Africa.

Opposing political forces divided the aristocrats of Assisi, including Clare's family, allies of the Holy Roman (but German) Emperor against the merchant class, including Francis' family, who wanted to shake off the yoke of imperial and aristocratic rule. Assisi was at war with itself in the early years of Francis' and Clare's lives, and a little later was at war with its neighbour and rival, the town of Perugia, visible on Assisi's horizon.

But there was also the holy war, the Crusade, that sent successive waves of knights, prophets, beggars and adventurers from Europe to the Near East.[10] Travelling minstrels sang the great deeds of the knightly class, and writers composed epics celebrating King Arthur and his Round Table, Tristan and Isolde, and the heroes of the *Roman de la Rose*.

The Crusades brought back to Assisi more than knights made famous by military exploits: they also brought leprosy. Hansen's disease, as it is known today, was rare in western Europe in the preceding centuries, but was endemic in the Near East. With the return of increasing numbers of Crusaders, merchants and pilgrims from the Holy Land, the disease spread at a rate that alarmed contemporary observers. Civil governments and church councils began to issue strict regulations to isolate those infected, and by the time Francis and Clare were born the town of Assisi had its own leper hospital, strictly quarantined, outside the city walls.

Those early years of the thirteenth century teemed with preachers, prophets and reformers, spreading a message of anxiety and expectation rendered more dramatic by the changing fortunes of the crusading armies. The anxiety was that of salvation: judgement was near; few would be saved; and only by following this teacher, that doctrine, or this other 'rule of life' could anyone hope for salvation. Alarmed by the message of popular preachers, church authorities grew increasingly anxious about the spread of heretical movements. The Cathars, or Albigensians, had created a church structure parallel to that of the Roman Church, with their bishops, priests and sacraments, in strongholds in the south of France, in Lombardy in northern Italy, and with outposts near Assisi.

FRANCIS

What we know of Francis' biography comes to us from the few indications in his writings, and from accounts of his life by his followers. *The Life of Saint Francis*, written by his contemporary Thomas of Celano, appeared in 1229, three years after his death. A second 'Life' (in fact, a mixture of different reminiscences), by the same author, composed some twenty years later, relied on written and oral accounts from the saint's early followers. These documents mix what we would call biographical information with popular motifs from legends of other saints (hagiography).[11] The following sketch of Francis' life will follow Thomas of Celano's outline, considered generally reliable.

Francis was born into a family of the rising merchant class of Assisi in 1181 or 1182. Baptised 'Giovanni', after St John the Baptist, he was known by his nickname 'Francesco', derived from the word for Frenchman. His father, Pietro di Bernardone, was a prosperous cloth merchant. His mother, named Pica in some sources, may have been French. After a youth marked at least by frivolity, if not actually gross sinfulness, Francis, after working in the family cloth business, wanted to advance in social rank by becoming a knight. Fighting on the Assisi side in the war with Perugia, he was captured and imprisoned. On his release, after a serious illness and another unsuccessful attempt at gaining knighthood in a military expedition in southern Italy, Francis began to undergo a conversion. He lived as a lay hermit, frequenting solitary places for prayer. He repaired churches, served lepers and began to attract followers. After the first group of 'brothers' numbered twelve, they asked for and received a verbal approval of their way of life from Pope Innocent III, who was doing the same for a number of new religious renewal movements at the time.

Francis undertook a number of preaching missions: first in Italy, later intending to go to Morocco via Spain (he turned back after suffering a serious illness); and to Egypt, during the Fifth Crusade, where he preached in the presence of the Islamic leader, Malek el-Kamil. Francis also continued seeking out solitary places for prayer, sometimes spending many months annually in his beloved hermitages in the mountains of central Italy. Toward the end of his life, in failing health, Francis withdrew from active leadership of the brotherhood, now called the Order of Lesser Brothers (or Friars Minor). Three years before his death (on the evening of 3 October 1226) he saw their Rule definitively approved by Pope Honorius III. Pope Gregory IX, the former Cardinal Hugolino, Bishop of Ostia, friend and counsellor of Francis, canonised him as a saint in 1228.

CLARE

We know about Clare primarily from her own writings, from the sworn testimony of witnesses at the proceedings preparing for her canonisation (called the 'Process'), and from *The Legend of St Clare*, by an anonymous contemporary author, one of Francis' followers.

As a young woman in a noble household, Clare grew up in an environment of contrasts: war and prayer; wealth and exile. Her father, Favarone di Offreduccio, was a prominent citizen of the town. Her mother, Ortolana, was a devout woman who travelled long distances on pilgrimages: to Rome, and to Mount

Gargano, the shrine of St Michael in southern Italy. Imitating her mother's example, Clare herself as a young woman helped a friend go on pilgrimage to the shrine of St James at Compostela in Spain.

The men in her family were knights, military men, and there were seven of them in the household, along with a household security guard, Giovanni di Ventura, later a witness at her canonisation proceedings. Her family's military and political alliances with other nobles in the area supported the Emperor, Frederick II. The merchants of the town wanted to be free of both the Emperor's 'occupation force' in the town and the nobles who supported it. This led to the civil war in Assisi, in which Francis himself may have taken part. The nobles and the Empire's forces were defeated in the conflict, and Clare, with her family, fled to nearby Perugia where she lived for several years in exile.

In her late teens, the customary age for marriage, she refused several potential husbands selected by her family. She saved food prepared for her to give to the poor, and took a special interest in those rebuilding churches in the area. In the house, she talked frequently about religious subjects, and her life of penance impressed even Giovanni, the security guard.[12]

She learned about Francis and his conversion. She could have heard him preach in the Cathedral of San Rufino, near her own home. She began to arrange meetings with him, accompanied by her friend Bona, but without her family's knowledge. Evidently she found what she was seeking in Francis' way of life. On the evening of Palm Sunday in 1211/12, at the age of eighteen, Clare left home secretly and, with her companion, went down the hill to the little church of St Mary of the Angels of the Porziuncola, in a wooded area near the city's leper hospital.

There Francis and his brothers met her. She had Francis cut her hair and put a veil on her head as a sign of her dedication to a 'converted' way of life under the protection of the Church. This was an odd sort of ritual: she was being admitted to a kind of religious consecration, by a man who really had no official authority, and into a movement that until that time had only men as members.

Francis and some of the brothers accompanied her that very evening to a nearby abbey of Benedictine nuns, San Paolo delle Badesse, protected by the patronage of the Pope himself. This proved to be a wise decision because, according to the story in her *Life*, her uncles came the next day in a fury and tried to drag her away.[13] They stopped only when she, holding onto the cloths of the altar in the abbey church, bared her head, revealing her cropped hair (the sign of being under church protection). She was claiming protection under the ancient right of sanctuary, a right jealously defended by the abbesses of San Paolo. Her relatives left her, for a time, and a few days later she moved to a community of women penitents, *bizzocche* or *beghine*, at Sant'Angelo in Panzo, on the hill above Assisi.

After some time at Sant'Angelo, and another confrontation with relatives when her sister Agnes joined her, Clare and her sister moved to a new home. With Francis' help, they took up residence at the little church of San Damiano, which he had repaired some years earlier. Once again, the actions of Francis and Clare seem puzzling: the church, though repaired by Francis, was certainly not his to offer, but was the property of the bishop. Here Clare and Agnes were joined by other women of the town, eventually numbering fifty, and Clare remained there for the next forty years until her death on 11 August 1253. She was canonised in 1255 by Pope Alexander IV.

FRANCIS AND FRANCISCAN SPIRITUALITY

To understand Franciscan spirituality we must begin with the spirituality of Francis himself, *il Poverello*, 'the little poor man' of Assisi. And to begin, we may again use some remarks from Martial Lekeux:

> The life of the Poverello may seem more cheerful and more peaceful than that of some of the other saints. But the

truth is that he was the saint of excesses: excess in sacrifice, excess in love: and it was by reason of his excesses that he held to the happy medium, because his disregard for moderation worked both ways, just as a scale insures better equilibrium the longer it is on both sides.

Francis is the saint of excesses and yet he is the saint with a smile, because he always fused the two. For him, penance was love, and sorrow 'perfect joy.' Using this standard, folly was wisdom and excess supreme moderation.[14]

We must make some sense of this 'excessive' saint if we wish to understand the beginnings and the permanent foundation of the Franciscan tradition. But understanding the tradition does not mean stopping with Francis. Otherwise we would have only the spirituality of an individual, not a 'tradition'. The word itself, from the Latin word for 'handing over', indicates that others received something from Francis. What was it? For his contemporaries, friends, companions, brothers and sisters, it was the experience of knowing Francis himself: he was the message. In a popular expression of the times, he taught them 'by word and example' (*verbo et exemplo*).[15] And, by their own testimony, he was for them a living example of what he taught: He edified his listeners by his example as well as his words; 'he made his whole body a tongue'; 'more than someone who prayed, he had become prayer': these are some of the descriptions of Francis recalled by Thomas of Celano.[16] That is, his whole person had become the message he was trying to communicate.

And what was that message? In a word, it was Jesus. To express it in such simple terms today may seem banal to us, or pious, or quaint. But for Francis, the discovery of Jesus, 'Our Lord Jesus Christ', was the ongoing revelation of his whole life in the twenty years after his conversion. In his early years he discovered Jesus as the one who led him among the lepers, and made their presence 'sweet' to him, rather than 'bitter'. He then discovered Jesus the preacher of conversion, announcing the reign of God. Over the years he began to see more clearly Jesus as the incarnate Son of God at Bethlehem, then as the Suffering Servant on Calvary; and finally, 'the Lord' of all things, raised up in glory after his death. And in this Lord, the glorified Son, he also understood the trinitarian God.

It is through 'the Lord Jesus Christ' that Francis understands Mary, the Church, the Scriptures, priesthood, the poor, his brothers and sisters, and all creatures. It is ultimately through and in Jesus that Francis even understands himself. Though he seldom used the title 'Christ' by itself to refer to Jesus, his spirituality, and that of the Franciscan tradition after him, has been characterised as 'Christocentric'.

> If there is one word which does complete justice to Franciscan theology and spirituality, it is 'Christocentric,' and they have this as their distinguishing feature, because the faith and holiness of St Francis were totally centered on Christ. In Jesus Christ the revelation is made to us of what the world, as a whole and in all its parts, means to God.[17]

CLARE AND FRANCISCAN SPIRITUALITY

Chief among the keepers and shapers of the Franciscan tradition is Clare of Assisi. She would describe herself as a *plantacula*, 'a little plant' of Francis, a term that has often led readers of her writings to assume a kind of inferiority. In context, however, Clare's name for herself indicates something different: she is separate but connected, rooted in the same soil of the gospel, sharing with Francis a 'form of life' she received from him as a gift from God. But the way in which she expresses her growing, intimate knowledge of 'following the footsteps of our Lord Jesus Christ' is uniquely her own. What unites Clare and Francis is not an identical experience of Christ, but different experiences of the same Christ.

In the last decade Clare has begun to assume, perhaps for the first time in the Franciscan tradition, the importance she deserves as the first interpreter of the Franciscan tradition. With the community of women who gathered around her, she served as an essential bridge between the earliest days of the Franciscan tradition and its communication to later generations. Since she outlived Francis by nearly thirty years – he died in 1226, she in 1253 – her interpretation of the 'founding moments' of the Franciscan school helped to shape the tradition in ways we are only now beginning to understand. One example may help to illustrate this important point. In the account of Clare's death, written within a year of the event, the description of people at her deathbed is illuminating. There is Leo, formerly secretary to Francis and one of his early companions. With him are Rufino and Angelo, two other early companions and personal friends. And these three are generally believed to be the most important sources for much of the knowledge we have of Francis' life. And, among all the early texts of the tradition, where do we find them, after Francis' death, all in the same place? Only at Clare's side. While the scene as it is described is probably historically accurate (the participants were all still living when Clare's *Life* was published), it is even more important for what it represents symbolically: Clare at the centre of the early companions, at the core of the tradition as it is being handed over to the next generation. For this reason, some authors today are beginning to speak of a 'Francis-Clarian' tradition. More than a disciple, Clare is also a creative architect of the tradition she lived.

GROWTH AND DEVELOPMENT

In the centuries following the deaths of Francis and Clare the tradition they established kept alive some great themes enunciated in their writings and exemplified in their lives, and neglected others, as we will see in the pages that follow. Controversies about the real intentions of the founders led to reforms and divisions, typifying the kind of anarchy that some have seen at the heart of this movement.

> The order which has been through the most crises is cer-
> tainly that of St Francis, a fine example of triumphant
> anarchy ... On the human level, it must be admitted that
> to have emerged victorious from so many crises is at least
> a sign of extraordinary vitality.[18]

Disputes over poverty rocked the Franciscan world from the
late thirteenth through the early fourteenth century. Various
reform movements championed their visions of an earlier age
of truly 'spiritual' Franciscan life, leading to divisions that in
part still mark contemporary Franciscan vocabulary: Conven-
tuals, observants, Capuchins, Reformed, Recollects and a host
of others.

The Franciscan tradition produced great theologians in the
thirteenth and fourteenth centuries, among whom Bonaventure and John Duns Scotus are the most important. And the
tradition has produced a wonderful and diverse crop of mystics
and spiritual writers, from Angela of Foligno in medieval
Umbria, to Benet of Canfield, a former English Puritan in
seventeenth-century France.

After more than a century of suppressions, persecutions and
gradual disintegration, at the end of the nineteenth century a
slow recovery began. All the components of the large Franciscan Family were again flourishing during the first half of the
twentieth century. With the call of the Second Vatican Council
for religious families to return to the charism of their founders,
the Franciscan tradition continued the long but fruitful process
of rediscovering Francis and Clare begun in the late 1800s.
And a study like this one would not have been possible without
what can only be called the explosion of interest in the two
saints from Assisi in the last twenty years.

THEMES OF THE FRANCISCAN TRADITION

After this brief overview of the history of the Franciscan tradition, a few words are in order about the themes of that
tradition. Each of the following chapters will examine one of

these: the incarnation; life in poverty; the lepers; the hermitages; the cross; and creation. In order of importance, the first
theme of Franciscan spirituality must be that of the incarnate
God. Though the topic recurs constantly in Christian spirituality, the particular emphasis given to the incarnation by the
Assisian saints relates it directly to their embrace of poverty
as a spiritual path.

Poverty, or 'living without grasping', marks the writings and
lives of both Francis and Clare. A key to their understanding
of Christ, poverty also became a source of division among their
followers.

People with Hansen's disease (leprosy) shaped Francis'
experience of human suffering in a way that led him to see
the suffering of Christ in vividly physical terms. Though their
presence was important in the spirituality of Francis himself,
the people with leprosy gradually 'disappear' in later Franciscan texts, until fairly recently.

Francis wrote a Rule for his brothers living in hermitages.
These places of solitude still symbolise the long tradition of
Franciscan contemplation. Championed especially by reform
movements, the places of retreat produced important writers
during the 'Golden Age' of sixteenth-century mysticism.

The cross, with its reference to suffering, death and glorifi-
cation, epitomises for these founders the depths of charity.
Clare's own vivid meditations of the 'Mirror suspended on the
wood of the Cross' reveal a good deal of her own mystical
identification with Christ. Francis, with his physical 'mirroring' of Christ's suffering, the 'stigmata' seen on his body,
became a popular saint in the Middle Ages for his 'conformity'
to the passion of Christ.

A well-known classic of medieval Italian religious poetry,
Francis' 'Canticle of the Creatures' or 'Canticle of Brother Sun',
opens a new chapter in the history of Christian spirituality.
Here are the seeds of a spirituality that embraces creation,
nature, the world, as a revelation of God, not a distraction.
Early biographers of the saint point to his unique relationship

of friendship, or kinship, with animals, plants and natural elements.

These few themes hardly cover the territory of Franciscan spirituality. Hopefully they will suggest some of its important landmarks. Each of the following chapters will examine the import of one of these themes in Francis, Clare and a few of their followers. In conclusion I will suggest some ways in which this 'anarchic' and lively tradition may help to satisfy a contemporary hunger for a liveable spirituality.

2. 'THE HUMILITY OF THE INCARNATION'

Today many people are searching for ways to connect their own everyday experience with the things they hear and read about 'spirituality'. Often the kind of spiritual teaching they receive seems disconnected from everyday concerns. It might even seem that one needs to live in a special place, to use special techniques, and have the leisure not to worry about day-to-day work and family responsibilities in order to achieve a kind of 'spiritual state'. The Franciscan tradition, with its emphasis on the incarnation, can provide an alternative view of spirituality, one firmly rooted in the ordinary events of human life.

For Francis, Clare and their brothers and sisters through the centuries the incarnation has been an unending source of inspiration and admiration. Angela of Foligno, a thirteenth-century lay penitent; Jacopone da Todi, poet, politician, and widower; Bonaventure of Bagnoregio and John Duns Scotus, theologians: their writings on the incarnation have helped to keep the Franciscan tradition faithful to this mystery.

THE GOOD GOD, THE TRINITY, AND THE IMAGE

Before speaking of the God who is incarnate, we need to have some general understanding of who God is. From Francis' own words, we gain some idea of the God he had in mind when he spoke about the incarnation: that God is good. Francis expresses this in the 'Praises of God' which he wrote out in his own hand for his companion, Brother Leo: 'You are good, all good, the highest good.' In the 'Praises to be said at all the

Hours' he writes: 'all good, supreme good, totally good, You Who alone are good'; 'fullness of Good, all good, every good, the true and supreme good, Who alone is Good'.[1] 'Good', 'Good', 'Good': God is good, and everything created is good. 'Peace and Good' ('*Pax et Bonum*') has been a Franciscan greeting for centuries. But it is more than that: it is a description of being with God.

Francis also speaks of this good God as Trinity: Creator, Redeemer and Saviour; Most High Father, beloved Son, and the most Holy Spirit the Paraclete. From the heart of this communion of persons the Word will be sent into the world.

> All-powerful, most holy most high and supreme God
> Holy and just Father
> Lord, King of heaven of earth
> we thank You for Yourself
> for through Your holy will
> and through Your only Son
> with the Holy Spirit
> You have created all things spiritual and corporal.[2]

From the 'most high' God all creation proceeds through the Son. Already here there is a strong link between the Son and all of creation. And this Son, through whom every spiritual and physical creature exists, comes as a creature among creatures, Jesus of Nazareth.

The only Son becomes human as a poor child, and lives in obscurity, without wealth or position. Francis recognised in this event of the incarnation the generosity of God, who does not hold onto anything, even divine status. In coming as a human being, the Son gives away exalted position and embraces with love human limitations, suffering, labour and even death. The life of Jesus is a moving picture (in both senses of the word) of God's life. In his First *Admonition*, Francis uses John's Gospel (14:6–9) to describe this: 'Philip, whoever sees me sees also my Father.'[3] In looking at Jesus Francis attempted to practise 'seeing' God in a creature.

When Francis looks attentively at Jesus, he discovers what

it means to be the image of God. So Francis also discovers what it means to be himself, because he is an image of God. He sums up this awareness in an Admonition:

> Be conscious, people, of the wondrous state in which the Lord God has placed you, for He created you and formed you to the image of His beloved Son according to the body, and to His likeness according to the spirit.[4]

In other words, the whole human person (body and spirit) reveals the image and likeness of the 'beloved Son'. In coming to know God, by looking at Jesus, Francis comes to know himself. But in another way, in knowing himself, Francis comes to see Jesus, and thus comes to know God.

This awareness, however, goes well beyond a form of introspective self-knowledge. The 'other', the brother, sister, neighbour, also reveals the image of the Son. And, as we will see later, 'brothers and sisters' can be human beings, or heavenly bodies, flowers and herbs, or the four cosmic elements.

In the earlier version of the Rule of the Lesser Brothers (dated to 1221) Francis writes in a similar vein:

> Almighty, Most High, Most Holy and Supreme God, holy and just Father, Lord, King of heaven and earth, we give you thanks for Yourself, because by Your holy will and through Your only Son in the Holy Spirit You have created all things, spiritual and corporal, and You placed us, made in Your image and likeness, in Paradise, and through our own fault we fell. We give You thanks because, as You created us by means of Your Son, so through Your true and holy love, with which You have loved us, You had the same true God and true man be born of the glorious, most blessed, holy, ever Virgin Mary, and by His cross, blood and death You have liberated and redeemed us.[5]

Here is the good God, the Trinity, and the Son as image of all things 'spiritual and corporal', a kind of summary of Francis' view of the incarnation, redemption and creation. In meditating on all those things created through the only Son, the late

Franciscan scholar Eric Doyle wrote a beautiful commentary, which is worth reproducing here in full, as a succinct statement of how the Christocentrism of Francis marks the Franciscan tradition across the centuries.

> [H]is devout love of the humanity of Jesus Christ brought him to understand that everything in heaven and on earth has been reconciled to God through Christ (Letter to a General Chapter). Francis reminds us all to realize the dignity God has bestowed on us: our body he formed and created in the image of his Son, our soul he made in his own likeness (Admonition V). This reflection is one of the most profound and far-reaching in the writings of St Francis. For it seems clear that he is asserting in it that the first Adam was created after the image of the second Adam, Jesus Christ. The body of the Incarnate Word, Jesus of Nazareth, was the blueprint for the bodies of the first human beings. A little after the time of St Francis, the learned doctor of the Order, Friar Alexander of Hales, explained that the image of God in whose likeness mankind was created, was the Saviour, who is the first-born of all creatures . . . For all their simplicity and clarity, these sentences of Francis just quoted, have a rich theological content. Contained in embryo is the Christocentric vision of the Franciscan school and even the doctrine of Christ's absolute primacy as formulated and expounded by John Duns Scotus.[6]

We will have the opportunity later to examine in more detail the way that this Christocentric vision of Francis developed in succeeding generations. For now, we turn from the words of Francis to his actions, the way in which he expressed externally, through some simple stage-props, his immersion in the wonder of the incarnation.

CHRISTMAS AT GRECCIO

Two weeks before Christmas in 1223, Francis was staying in the little hillside hermitage near the town of Greccio, south of Assisi. According to his contemporary, Brother Thomas of Celano, Francis called a friend of his, named Giovanni, to help him in preparing a special celebration of the forthcoming feast. He asked that animals and hay be brought to a cave at the hermitage, so that a scene could be prepared to show the people of the town and his own brothers the physical conditions of the birth of Jesus.

He wanted people to be able to experience what it was like for the Son of God to be born in a stable, surrounded by the ox and ass, straw and cold. Francis' brothers and the people of the town of Greccio gathered in the cave on Christmas Eve, lighting up the night with torches, singing hymns, with a priest celebrating Mass on an altar arranged over the manger. Francis himself, 'dressed as a Levite', sang the Gospel 'in a beautiful voice', and preached, full of emotion. Thomas tells us that it seemed as if the infant Jesus, long forgotten in the hearts of the people, came to life that night. And all of creation, the trees and stones of the surrounding mountainside, echoed the praises sung by the people.[7]

This simple kind of nativity scene was destined to be spread by Franciscans throughout the world as they moved out from Assisi in the following centuries. It is by now a familiar feature of Christmas celebrations throughout the world. Though it has suffered its share of commercialisation, and its significance has sometimes become purely sentimental, at its origins the nativity scene was a striking affirmation of God's entry into the mundane, everyday life of poor people, the world of creatures, the world of straw and rocks.

THE NATIVITY, THE EUCHARIST, AND THE VIRGIN

What impressed Francis so deeply about the feast of Christ's birth was its simplicity, humility and poverty. In many ways

Christmas helped to form Francis' notion of who God is.
Brother Thomas speaks of Francis' profound grasp of the
'humility of the Incarnation'.[8] In his own words, Francis speaks
of this understanding:

> Through his angel, Saint Gabriel, the most high Father in
> heaven announced this Word of the Father – so worthy, so
> holy and glorious – in the womb of the holy and glorious
> Virgin Mary, from which He received the flesh of humanity
> and our frailty. Though He was rich beyond all other
> things, in this world He, together with the most blessed
> Virgin, His mother, willed to choose poverty.[9]

What the Christmas Eve celebration at Greccio depicts is a
choice: the Divine Word chooses poverty voluntarily as a form
of life, together with Mary. The drama of this choice is evoked
by the setting, bare and cold, on a hillside outside the town,
with only animals and other people for warmth. Thomas tells
us that Francis wanted the people of Greccio and his own
brothers to see with their own eyes the kind of circumstances
the gospel describes about the birth of Jesus, and 'the incon-
veniences of his infant needs'. 'There simplicity was honored,
poverty was exalted, humility was commended, and Greccio
was made, as it were, a new Bethlehem.'[10]

That triad of simplicity, poverty and humility were, for
Francis, hallmarks of the whole life of Jesus, a life he wished
to follow. That same triad characterised the celebration of the
Eucharist, not only at the manger in the cave at Greccio, but
every Eucharist. It is as if every time the Mass was celebrated
Francis saw the choice of the incarnation reaffirmed. In a
letter to all his brothers, perhaps written in 1224, a year after
the Christmas feast at Greccio, he wrote:

> O admirable heights and sublime lowliness!
> O sublime humility!
> O humble sublimity!
> That the Lord of the universe,
>   God and the Son of God,

so humbles Himself
that for our salvation
He hides Himself under the little form of bread!
Look, brothers, at the humility of God
and pour out your hearts before Him!
Humble yourselves, as well,
    that you may be exalted by Him.[11]

The brothers are urged to see the same scenario of incarnation, the choice of humility and poverty, every time they participate in the Eucharist. The 'little form' of bread, so unremarkable in itself, is the 'hiding place' of the Son of God. As his reasoning goes, Francis sees this dynamic of infinity contained in the finite as 'the humility of God', a humility not only to be admired, but also to be imitated: 'humble yourselves', that is, 'be like God'.

Mary is, in Francis' words, *virgo ecclesia facta*, 'the virgin made church'.[12] Like Jesus, Mary is poor: 'In this world He, together with the most blessed Virgin, His mother, willed to choose poverty.'[13] In exhorting his brothers not to be ashamed when need forces them to beg from door to door, he invokes the figure of Mary with that of Jesus again, as an example of humility and poverty: 'He was a poor man and lived on alms, He and the Blessed Virgin and His disciples.'[14] The context of poverty in which Jesus is born is also the context of Mary's own life, and that of all of the disciples of Jesus. It is not merely an accident: it is a free choice, an embrace of the way of life that will lead to exaltation.

The Feast of Christmas, the celebration of the Eucharist, the example of Mary: each of these points Francis toward the poverty and humility of God revealed in Jesus. If the incarnation, the 'in-humaning' and 'in-mattering' of the Son of God can be summed up in a word within the Franciscan School, that word would be 'poverty'.

BONAVENTURE

Friar, theologian, diplomat, bishop, cardinal: Bonaventure of Bagnoregio (d. 1274) was all of these, and successor of Francis as seventh Minister General of the Lesser Brothers. More than anyone else, this energetic intellectual, law-maker and organiser put into systematic form insights he derived from his knowledge of Francis. Born in Italy a few years before Francis died, he joined the friars in 1243, while he was a student in Paris, and knew the life and words of the founder through reading, liturgy and story-telling. He was part of that 'new generation' of Franciscans who had not known Francis personally (he was only nine years old when Francis died). Clare died just as he was finishing his studies in Paris, in 1253, though some of Francis' other early companions were still living when Bonaventure was elected Minister General in 1257: Angelo (d. 1258); Giles (d. 1262); Rufino (d. 1271); and Leo (d. 1271). Bonaventure is a 'bridge' figure, translating Francis' insights (he hardly mentions Clare) for later generations. In this way Bonaventure may be considered one of the great creators of the 'Franciscan School' of spirituality as an identifiable body of beliefs and practices.

A wonderful text illustrating Bonaventure's understanding of the incarnation is a Christmas sermon he composed, and probably delivered to the university community while he was teaching in Paris. He begins with his text: 'The Word was made flesh' (John 1:14), and then moves immediately to identifying that proclamation of the incarnation with a theme dear to Francis:

> These words give expression to that heavenly mystery and that admirable sacrament, that magnificent work of infinite kindness which consists in the fact that the eternal God has humbly bent down and lifted the dust of our nature into unity with His own person.[15]

Here, as in the writings of Francis and Clare, the words 'humbly bent down' remind us of the Franciscan emphasis on the incarnation as an expression of humility. Reflecting on the great hymn in the Letter to the Philippians ('he emptied himself'; 'he humbled himself'), Bonaventure says that 'in this Word made flesh we find the self-emptying of that exalted nature in One who humbled Himself'.[16]

In developing another facet of the incarnation, he presents the body of Christ as the resolution of the great speculative questions of Christian mysticism in his classic work of mystical theology, *The Soul's Journey into God*. 'Passing over' even the mind itself, the contemplative sees Christ, and specifically Christ on the cross, as 'the way and door', the 'ladder and the vehicle',[17] the way out of the impasses of reconciling apparently opposite dimensions of Christian religious experience (Creator and creature; infinite and finite; divine and human). That is, through the incarnation, God's own action has resolved in fact problems which remain puzzling in theory.

And this wonderful event of the incarnation fulfils and heals the work of creation: 'Indeed, I would say that He has created all things in his uncreated Word, and recreated all things in the Incarnate Word.'[18] The uncreated Word created human beings in the beginning, and the incarnate Word redeems them.[19] Creation and redemption both have their origin in the Word. These are not two disconnected realities, but the work of the same Creator and Redeemer, the eternal Word made flesh out of love for us.

ANGELA OF FOLIGNO

Along with Francis and his brothers, Clare and her sisters, the early Franciscan movement also included other men and women who followed a similar form of gospel life. These are the Brothers and Sisters of Penance, later called the 'Third Order', today known as the Secular Franciscan Order. Married or single, living in their own homes, or in small groups or as solitaries, these lay penitents have made their own unique contributions to Franciscan spirituality.

Angela of Foligno (d. 1309), an early member of the Order

of Penance, has left us an especially rich legacy of writing on her personal religious experience. A member of the wealthy aristocracy of Foligno, an important town south of Assisi, Angela describes her early life as filled with vanity and sin. She had married, though we do not know her husband's name, and had at least two children. Though she was apparently a believing Christian in her early years, she later described her early religiosity as shallow and artificial. In her early forties she began to undergo a profound religious conversion, during which she was strongly influenced by the figure of St Francis, who had died several years before she was born. After the death of her husband and her children within a brief period, she dedicated herself more intensely to the religious quest. Following the same gospel injunction that had moved Francis and Clare, Angela began to sell her considerable properties, giving the proceeds to the poor. She cared for the sick, notably people with leprosy, and embraced a life of penitence and prayer in her home town, accompanied by a faithful friend and companion.

In her spiritual autobiography, known as the *Memorial*,[20] Angela recounts for her spiritual director the stages of her spiritual journey. In the companion piece, the *Instructions*, she offers to a group of disciples (including friars) her teaching on various aspects of the Christian life, particularly in regard to prayer. Her profound influence on these disciples eventually gained her the title of 'Teacher of Theologians' (*magistra theologorum*).

Adding to the Franciscan tradition of reflection on the mystery of the incarnation, Angela's *Memorial* gives us vivid descriptions of her personal assimilation of this favourite theme of the Franciscan School.

> Once I was meditating on the poverty of the Son of God incarnate. I saw his poverty – its greatness was demonstrated to my heart, to the extent that he wished me to see it – and I saw those for whom he had made himself poor . . . God wanted to demonstrate to me even more of

his poverty. And I saw him poor of friends and relatives. I even saw him poor of himself and so poor that he seemed powerless to help himself. It is sometimes said that the divine power was then hidden out of humility. But even if this has been said, I say that God's power was not hidden then, because he himself has taught me otherwise. From this vision of the poverty of the Son of God, I experienced and felt an even greater sorrow than before, for in it I recognized so much of my own pride that joy was no longer possible.[21]

Further on in the *Memorial* Angela returns to this connection between the incarnation and poverty, one so clearly present in the writings of Francis and Clare. In describing one of her frequent conversations with God, the scribe recording Angela's experiences (Brother 'A') relates the following:

Christ's faithful one also said that God had spoken to her and from him she had heard poverty praised as such a lofty teaching and such a great good that it totally exceeds our capacity to understand it. God had told her: 'If poverty were not such a great good, I would not have loved it. And if it were not so noble I would not have assumed it.'[22]

Angela frequently describes her intense religious experiences in vividly physical, sensual language, full of affection. She experiences the bodiliness of Christ as the means of her union with him. As the following passage illustrates, hers is an incarnate experience of that union.

On Holy Saturday . . . in a state of ecstasy, she found herself in the sepulcher with Christ. She said she had first of all kissed Christ's breast – and saw that he lay dead, with his eyes closed – then she kissed his mouth, from which, she added, a delightful fragrance emanated, one impossible to describe. This moment lasted only a short while. Afterward, she placed her cheek on Christ's own and he, in turn, placed his hand on her other cheek pressing her closely to him. At that moment, Christ's faithful one heard him telling her: 'Before I was laid in the sepulcher, I held you this tightly to me.'[23]

After describing the experience of 'standing or lying in the midst of the Trinity', in which 'I see with such darkness', Angela connects this ineffable experience with the incarnate Christ:

> When I am in that darkness I do not remember anything about anything human, or the God-man, or anything which has form. Nevertheless, I see all and I see nothing. As what I have spoken of withdraws and stays with me, I see the God-man. He draws my soul with great gentleness and he sometimes says to me: 'You are I and I am you.' I see, then, those eyes and that face so gracious and attractive as he leans to embrace me. In short, what proceeds from those eyes and that face is what I said that I saw in that previous darkness which comes from within, and which delights me so that I can say nothing about it.[24]

This enigmatic description unites two aspects of Christian mysticism, sometimes considered as opposites, sometimes as complements to each other. These are the so-called apophatic and kataphatic approaches. Apophatic mysticism emphasises the indescribable nature of religious experience, while the kataphatic pushes language, metaphor and description to their limits in trying to describe that experience. In the *Memorial*, Angela seems to move easily between the two, from darkness to Christ, then glimpsing that same darkness she had experienced coming 'from within' her now coming from the incarnate, bodily Christ, his eyes and face. This single passage depicts a resolution of the tension between the visible and the invisible, the describable and the indescribable. And that resolution occurs in the body, that of Angela and that of Christ. Angela affirms 'since that time there has not been a day or a night in which I did not continually experience this joy of the humanity of Christ'. And that joy makes her want 'to sing and praise', in other words, to break out in a *laude*, a type of popular thirteenth-century religious hymn. The lyrics of the *laude* she quotes are these:

> I praise you God my beloved;
> I have made your cross my bed.
> For a pillow or cushion,
> I have found poverty,
> and for other parts of the bed,
> suffering and contempt to rest on.[25]

Asked to explain this metaphor of the bed, Angela responds:

> This bed is my bed to rest on because on it Christ was born, lived, and died. Even before man sinned, God the Father loved this bed and its company (poverty, suffering and contempt) so much that he granted it to his Son.[26]

In her meditation on the 'bed' of the cross, with poverty, suffering and contempt as its furnishings, Angela provides a link between language that can be found in Clare ('we had no fear of poverty, hard work, suffering, shame, or the contempt of the world'[27]) and the profound christological affirmation of John Duns Scotus years later, that Christ would have come even if Adam had not sinned. In Angela's words, 'even before man sinned', God loved the conditions associated with the cross-bed.

While not schooled in the formal philosophy or theology of her time, Angela made a profound impression on her group of disciples, some of whom had formal education in those disciplines, like Ubertino da Casale, a leading spokesman for the ideals of the 'spirituals', a reform group with the Lesser Brothers. Her bodily, incarnate mysticism has intrigued scholars dedicated to the study of Christian mysticism, such as Evelyn Underhill.[28]

JACOPONE DA TODI

He was a poet, notary, widower, penitent, friar and political prisoner. At times exasperating for his sarcasm, at other

moments a stirring writer of lyrical mysticism, Jacopone da
Todi (d. 1306) shows us another side of the Franciscan School,
that of the popular preacher, the market-place actor and min-
strel, and the intensely political contemplative. He was a man
of aristocratic heritage who had studied at the University of
Bologna, later marrying Vanna di Bernardino, and working as
a *notaio*, a kind of lawyer-notary-consultant. After Vanna's
death he embraced the life of a lay penitent for ten years
before joining the Lesser Brothers in 1278, just four years after
Bonaventure's death. From 1297 until 1303 he was in prison,
accused of conspiring in a plot to overthrow a pope he
thoroughly disliked, Boniface VIII, whom he thought was probably the Antichrist. The example of Francis and the writings
of Bonaventure shaped much of his religious outlook,
expressed in *lodi*, 'lauds' or 'praises', popular religious poems
adaptable for singing.[29]

Two of the Lauds are dedicated especially to the theme of
the incarnation. In the opening strophes of Laud 64, 'A Canticle
of the Nativity', Jacopone uses singing and musical notation,
along with the medieval scribe's familiar work, as metaphors
of the incarnation.

> A new canticle I hear,
> To dry the tears of the afflicted!
>
> I hear it begin with a piercing tone,
> Whence it slowly descends several octaves,
> For it celebrates the coming of the Word. Never was heard
> A descending scale of such exquisite melody!
>
> The joyous chorus is that of angels
> Singing sweet songs around the manger
> Before the Christ Child,
> The Word Incarnate.
>
> 'Glory to God in the highest,' they sing,
> 'And peace on earth –

An end to war and to all evils;
Praise and bless the Infant adored!'

The sacred notes, I see,
Are inscribed on parchment, skin of the lamb;
In the Lamb – our penetrating eye discerns –
Is all song, whether solo or choral.

The hand that moves across the page
Is the hand of God,
And it is God in His mercy
Who teaches us to sing.[30]

The poem evokes the incarnation with a dramatic high-pitched note, then dropping, octave by octave: the theme of the descent of the Son of God who becomes the Son of Mary. In his description of the manger, we already notice the spreading influence of the early Franciscan representations of the birth of Christ in nativity scenes, like that of Francis at Greccio. Jacopone then shifts his attention from singing voices to the musical score itself. Here the flesh, the human body of the child Jesus, the Lamb of God, finds its symbol in the material 'lambskin', the parchment sheet used for writing music in the thirteenth century. We 'sight-read' that musical score by contemplating the incarnation, learning from God, the ultimate choirmaster, how to sing, responding to the mystery we read in the body of Christ.

In Laud 65, 'Second Canticle of the Nativity', Jacopone expresses poetically that great theme of the Franciscan School, the poverty of the incarnation.

In place of Your glorious throne,
A manger and a little straw;
In place of a starry crown,
Poor swaddling clothes
And the warm breath of an ox and an ass;
In place of a glorious court, Mary and Joseph.

Were these the actions of someone drunk, or out of his senses?
How could You abdicate kingdom and riches,
A renunciation that verges on madness?
Did someone promise You other and greater treasure?
O measureless love that would cede
Such glory as Yours for such humble estate![31]

This is only one of many places where Jacopone compares the free choice of the incarnation to madness on the part of the Son. The madness of love is the poet's explanation for the choice to renounce the splendours of heaven, compared to a splendid, medieval royal court, and to accept the humble conditions of the manger at Bethlehem.

Love, poverty, humility: these three words recur in the Lauds of Jacopone with some frequency, and they echo the words used by Francis and Clare to describe the incarnation. The Franciscan tradition of spirituality consists of such echoes, reverberations of a similar musical theme, with variations in different composers.

Perhaps the most important author within that tradition of reflection on the incarnation is the philosopher and theologian, John Duns Scotus, who uses the language of technical, Scholastic theology, rather than the poetic language of Jacopone, to express that same mystery.

SCOTUS AND THE MOTIVE OF THE INCARNATION

John Duns Scotus (d. 1308) lived and taught in the lively theological milieux of Oxford and Paris before his untimely death, at the age of forty-four, in Cologne. His philosophical and theological writings would usually not appear in collections of texts on spirituality, but their long-term effect was to shape Franciscan spirituality for centuries. And among these writings, his reflections on the incarnation have had the greatest influence on that tradition.[32]

The reason for the incarnation according to Scotus is the love which is intrinsic to God's own being. Since the incarnation is

God's 'greatest work', it can hardly be explained as something occasioned by outside influences, something 'incidental'.[33] In the technical language of his day, Scotus argued that 'it is not likely that the highest good in the whole of creation is something that merely happened by chance, and happened only because of some lesser good'.[34] The grandeur of the incarnation cannot be an afterthought on the part of God, decreed as a response to the problem of human sin. Frederick Faber, the popular spiritual writer of the mid-nineteenth century, put it in these simple terms:

> If Christ was decreed after us, and because of us, and only to redeem us, these three monstrous consequences follow; first, that Christ would owe us a debt of gratitude; secondly, that we should in certain respects be more excellent than he; and thirdly, that sin was necessary to his existence.[35]

In our own language, we might explain this in the following way. The incarnation of the Word, the Son, is the highest good, the supreme expression of God's love, which is the inner identity of God. By comparison with the infinite Love revealed in the incarnation, correcting the effects of the sin of Adam and Eve is a 'lesser good'. If the incarnation was provoked by human sin, then the magnificence of the solution is out of proportion to the size of the problem. And if humans had *not* sinned, there would be no need for the incarnation (one of Father Faber's 'monstrous consequences').

Scotus proposed his own reasons for the coming of Christ in this way: 'I say that the incarnation of Christ was not foreseen as occasioned by sin, but was immediately foreseen from all eternity by God as a good more proximate to the end.'[36] This statement, in medieval theological language, may need some translation. The 'end' here refers to God's purpose or goal for the whole of creation. The goal, according to Scotus, is the sharing of God's own life, one so fruitful that it constantly seeks expression. The ultimate goal ('end') must be sharing the life of the Trinity itself. Within the Trinity, the Son or

Word, is the centre or heart, the 'way into' the Trinity. As the self-diffusive love of God is expressed in the act of creation, the Son is the Image or Form for everything God creates. Now, if God's ultimate goal for creation is participation in divine life itself, the incarnation of the Son is a 'good' very close to the goal ('more proximate to the end'). Why? Because Christ becomes the bridge, the middle member, linking the creation (including humans) to the inner life of God. Christ becomes the necessary gate or way into God's life, the ultimate goal intended for all creation.

In reviewing the previous theological tradition, Scotus considers what the 'authorities' (scriptural and patristic authors) said on the subject, and concludes that 'all the authorities can be explained in this way: Christ would not have come *as Redeemer* if the first person had not fallen.'[37] That is not the same as saying 'Christ would not have come'. The *mode* of the incarnation was affected by human sin (Christ came also to redeem); but the *motive* was a free act of love.

> Since humans could have been redeemed in another way, but nevertheless [Christ] chose to redeem them in that way by an act of his free will, we are greatly indebted to him . . . I believe he did this chiefly to draw us to his love, and because he wanted us to cling more closely to God.[38]

Scotus himself did not develop these insights in works that we would consider popular works of spirituality. His language, and his ideas themselves, gained him the title of the 'Subtle Doctor'. But as his works spread throughout the Franciscan schools of the fourteenth century, they helped to give Franciscan spirituality a theological language to express intuitions that remained inchoate in the writings of Francis and Clare: the incarnation as the greatest expression of love, and Christ's death as the ultimate, free act of that love.

MARY AS THE FULL IMAGE OF HUMANITY

When the doctrine of the Immaculate Conception was solemnly proclaimed on 8 December 1854, many Franciscans saw the event as an honour, not only to Mary, but also to Scotus. As a corollary of his view of Christ, incarnate because of love, not because of sin, he maintained that Mary of Nazareth was conceived without sin. Without analysing here the various texts of Scotus about Mary, I would like to offer a simple explanation of some of his thinking about the notion of Mary as the fully human person.[39]

It often seems that when we speak of Mary's conception without sin we imply that something is 'missing' in her, namely 'original sin'. But we also say that sin is the *lack* of something: it is *not being* like God. What this doctrine celebrates is that Mary is fully and clearly what a human person is meant to be, what all of us are created to be: clear images of God. To understand the beauty of this approach, we may take a moment to look at Scotus' view of the human person in Christ.

Because Scotus always considered Christ first, he saw the person as the living image of the Word incarnate. In Scotus' view (we call this the Primacy of Christ or Christocentrism) creation is modelled on the humanity of Christ. That human person is the goal of creation. Everything is made through him, for him, and in him. He is really Adam, the first Adam. The Adam of Genesis is his image. The beginning of Genesis, the story of the world and humanity before sin, is the image of who Christ is.

God plans all things in view of the human form of the Son, Christ, and intends the Son to be 'born of woman'. To use the mundane metaphor of making a plan, we could say that after deciding that the Son shall be incarnate as a human, the trinitarian God next chose the woman who will be invited to share her humanity with God.

What kind of human being shall she be? The clearest image of the Son, the most appropriate: she will be *fully* human. And so she was, as God intended, a woman who lived as a fully human person. Only now can we move to the beginning of Genesis. God's logic moves backwards, it seems, from one point of view. God starts with the New Testament and then goes to the beginning of the Old Testament: Christmas comes logically before creation. Christ precedes Adam, and Mary precedes Eve. The medieval Scholastics had a Latin phrase for this: *primum in intentione, ultimum in executione*, 'the thing you first intended is the last thing completed'.

Following this logic, Christ comes first, then Mary, then Adam and Eve. As we read the Genesis story, we see the full God-image of Adam and Eve change, as they freely choose to be something else than God's full image. That decision makes them less who they really are as human persons; it is the denial of full humanity, but it was their choice and God does not prevent them from making it. To take away their freedom would make them incomplete images of the free Son.

We call that choice 'original sin', and according to the Scriptures, that choice has an impact in the next generation, with Cain and Abel, and the next and the next, through Noah to Abraham to Moses to David to Solomon, to our own day.

But the image of God is not lost, it is obscured. It is harder to see true humanity, Christ's humanity, but the image, tarnished, is still there.

With the conception of Mary, the Great Plan, the book before Genesis, begins. A human person is conceived in *full* humanity. Mary is who we really are: freely, fully, soul and body, her humanity *for* Christ, *in* Christ, *of* Christ.

It would be better to give a different name to this doctrine. It is the doctrine of Mary-who-was-conceived-without-sin. But why define someone by what they are *not*? This could be named the doctine of Mary, Fully Human. For in God's logic, that is what all of us are to be, ultimately, and what we *are* in God's design.

Was she conceived without sin? I saw this answer in the crude lettering on a shrine at the friary of Belmonte in Northern Italy. Mary is painted there, Scotus on the left beside her crude image and Francis on the right. Above her, the words

badly lettered, is a Scotist's explanation of God's reasons –
Potuit, Decuit, ergo Fecit: 'It could be done, it should be done,
so God did it.' A traditional hymn, sung on Saturday evenings
in Franciscan houses around the world, has brought this
Scotistic message home over the centuries:

Tota pulchra es, Maria	Mary, you are the most beautiful
Et macula originalis	No stain from the beginning
Non est in te.	is in you.
Tu, gloria Ierusalem!	You, glory of Jerusalem!
Tu, laetitia Israel!	You, Israel's joy!
Tu, honorificentia populi nostri!	You, our people's pride!
Tu, advocata peccatorum!	You, sinners' advocate!
Oh, Maria! Oh, Maria!	Oh, Mary, oh Mary!
Virgo prudentissima,	Wise virgin
Mater clementissima,	Merciful mother,
Ora pro nobis.	Pray for us,
Intercede pro nobis	Intercede for us,
Ad Dominum Iesum Christum.	With the Lord, Jesus Christ.

3. 'THE POVERTY AND HUMILITY OF OUR LORD JESUS CHRIST'

Lady, holy Poverty, may the Lord protect you
with your sister, holy Humility. (Francis)[1]

O God-centered poverty,
   whom the Lord Jesus Christ
   Who ruled and now rules heaven and earth,
   Who spoke and things were made,
   condescended to embrace before all else. (Clare)[2]

The Franciscan tradition in Christian spirituality has assigned extraordinary importance to poverty as integral to the practice of Christian discipleship. Its importance is well attested in all the principal spiritual writers of the tradition, and it has sparked both reform and division in the Franciscan movement over eight centuries.[3]

Poverty, as a characteristic of Jesus, was one of the organising principles of the spirituality of Francis himself. Clare, over four decades, constantly insisted on its primacy in her life with her sisters and recommended it ardently to others. In succeeding generations it inspired authors like Angela of Foligno, her disciple, Ubertino da Casale, and many others to strive, even against fierce opposition, to follow a spiritual path that many others found difficult to understand or accept.

To understand the central place that poverty occupies in the Franciscan tradition, we will begin with the example of Francis and Clare and then explore the development of the tradition in the generations that succeeded them.

FRANCIS: 'VIVERE SINE PROPRIO'

In his *Testament* Francis insists that the Lord revealed to him the 'form of life' he was to live.[4] This way of living is fundamentally 'to observe the Holy Gospel of Our Lord Jesus Christ', as he wrote at the beginning of the Rule. And that included living 'without anything of one's own' (*vivere sine proprio*).[5]

The phrase occurs frequently in Francis' writings, especially in his *Admonitions*, which can be read as a commentary on this expression. These are mostly brief sayings, like those of the Desert Fathers of early Christian monasticism. They were most likely written by others who heard them when Francis addressed gatherings of his brothers (the chapters held each year). The various ways in which living *sine proprio* recurs in these sayings echo words of Francis from his other writings.

What does this 'non-possessing' life mean? Primarily, it means living as a disciple, following the teaching of the Beatitudes. Those who live without anything of their own are 'the poor in spirit; theirs is the Kingdom of heaven' (Matthew 5:3).[6] They live 'according to the Spirit'. The opposite of this way of living is 'to appropriate', to claim things as one's own. And those who live in this way live 'according to the flesh'.

This attitude of radical non-possessing touches every part of human life, from our own will to the doing of good works. We would 'repeat the sin of our first parents' if we seek to 'appropriate' our own will.[7] None of the brothers is to 'appropriate' a position of authority.[8] Those who study sacred Scripture are not to use their knowledge to accumulate riches.[9] No brother is to appropriate anger or disturbances[10] or scandal for wrongs done.[11]

The *Admonitions* also give us Francis' reasons for refusing to appropriate anything: it is the 'Most High' who 'says and does' every good thing.[12] All that is good belongs to the Most High alone, and to appropriate to ourselves anything is 'blasphemy', attributing to ourselves what belongs to God. Put in different terms, for Francis, everything was a gift. To pretend that anything that we have or are belongs to us as 'property' is a kind of *lèse majesté*, an affront to God who is 'All Good' and gives 'every good thing'.

The 'All Good' God, Father, Son and Spirit, far from holding on jealously to all good gifts, gives generously, even divine life itself. Francis sees this good God when he looks at Jesus. Quoting John's Gospel (14:6–9) at the beginning of the *Admonitions*, he recalls that 'the Lord Jesus' said to Philip, 'whoever sees me sees my Father'. Using the Eucharist as his point of reference, Francis declares that 'every day' this same Jesus 'descends' from the Father into the hands of the priest, and comes to us 'in humble appearance', as he did when he 'descended from the royal throne' into the 'womb of the Virgin'.[13]

In the incarnation, as in the Eucharist, Francis sees 'the Lord Jesus Christ' (and therefore the 'most holy Father'). Instead of holding onto high status and power ('the royal throne') this Lord chooses to 'descend', to be among people 'in humble appearance'. For Francis, poverty begins with the example of God, seen in Jesus. Two texts of St Paul express this 'poverty of God' as Francis perceived it, one from the Letter to the Philippians, another from the Second Letter to the Corinthians:

> Have this mind among you, which was in Christ Jesus who, though he was in the form of God, did not count equality with God something to be grasped, but emptied himself, taking the form of a servant, and being born in human likeness. And being found in human form he humbled himself, becoming obedient unto death, even death on a cross. Therefore God has highly exalted him and bestowed on him the name above every name, that at the name of Jesus every knee should bend, in heaven, on earth and under the earth, and every tongue confess that Jesus Christ is Lord, to the glory of God the Father. (Philippians 2:5–11)

> ... our Lord Jesus Christ, though he was rich, for your

sake he became poor, so that by his poverty you might become rich. (2 Corinthians 8:9)

The poverty of Francis is a response to Christ Jesus, who did not 'grasp' or cling to divine status, but let go of it to be among humans as a servant. This Jesus who was born in lowly status, lived as a poor man and died on the cross, the ultimate 'letting go'. Since he is 'the Way, the Truth, and the Life' (John 14:6), as Francis states,[14] the way into God is the way of relinquishment, without grasping or appropriating anything.

Without this christological understanding, poverty becomes a penitential practice in its own right, simply a means of ascetical discipline or moral self-improvement. And to understand poverty primarily as a matter of having fewer of these, or less of that, counting and measuring with the eye of a spiritual accountant, makes a caricature out of Francis' vision.

In the Rule of the Lesser Brothers, Chapter Six expresses this vision:

The brothers shall claim nothing as their own: neither a house, nor a place, nor anything. As pilgrims and strangers [1 Peter 2:1] in this world, serving the Lord in poverty and humility, let them confidently seek alms. Nor should they be ashamed, because the Lord made himself poor [cf. 2 Corinthians 8:9] for us in this world. My dearest brothers, this is the excellency of the most high poverty, that makes you heirs and kings of the kingdom of heaven, making you poor in things but rich in virtues. Let this be your portion that leads you to the land of the living [Psalm 141:6]. Dearest brothers, totally joined to this poverty, do not wish to have anything else under heaven, forever, in the name of our Lord Jesus Christ.[15]

The promise of this 'most high poverty' is life, abundance, the kingdom of heaven, life with Christ. Francis, the former merchant, sold all he had to possess this treasure; and in the Rule required all those joining the brothers to do the same. Those who want to accept 'this life' should be sent to the

ministers (superiors), who shall tell them 'the word of the Holy
Gospel', namely that they 'go and sell all they have and strive
to give it to the poor'.[16] The word of the gospel here is from
Matthew 19:21, where the young man with many possessions
hears the words of Jesus: 'If you would be perfect, go, sell what
you possess and give to the poor, and you will have treasure
in heaven, and come, follow me.'[17]

Francis saw the 'life according to the Holy Gospel' as necessarily including this transaction, selling and giving, as a
concrete participation in the dynamic of Christ 'who was rich
and made himself poor' for humanity. Once again, the letting
go is not for its own sake, as a moral virtue; it is a letting go
for the sake of the poor, modelled on the generous self-giving
of God seen in the birth, life, ministry, death and resurrection of Jesus.

CLARE AND THE 'PRIVILEGE OF POVERTY'

Clare once characterised herself as the *plantacula* of Francis.
Literally, the word means 'little plant', and has given rise to
some sentimental interpretations of Clare as a 'shrinking
violet', or a fragile flower kept under glass in the enclosure of
San Damiano. Even a superficial glance at the writings and
life of Clare would betray that interpretation. She tenaciously
strove to follow a call that was opposed, even violently, by men
in her family. She advised other women to remain firm in their
intention to follow the same way of life she followed, no matter
what advice they received from others. And she insisted, over
forty years, on a privilege she treasured, the 'privilege of
poverty'. The reason for her expression 'little plant', as we will
see, refers to her sharing the form of life lived by Francis and
his brothers, especially in regard to the 'poverty of Our Lord
Jesus Christ'.

In her Testament Clare speaks fervently of 'the love of the
Lord Who was poor as He lay in the crib, poor as He lived in
the world, Who remained naked on the cross'.[18] She sees the
whole life of Jesus as a life marked by poverty, from the

moment of the incarnation, through the adult years of labour and ministry, to the time of his death. To 'follow the footsteps' of Jesus, that is, to be a disciple, means to embrace the kind of life he led, one of poverty.

For Clare, her life and that of her sisters was to be a 'mirror' for the world, and an example to other sisters whom the Lord calls to their way of life.[19] The image of the mirror in Clare's writings can help us to understand why poverty was so important to her: the mirror is the poor Jesus.

Clare used the image of a medieval mirror to talk about Jesus. The rounded, polished metal disc with its uneven reflection was very different from today's flat, smooth mirrors. Looking first at the edges of the mirror, then gradually shifting her gaze to its centre, she turned the surface of the mirror into a symbol of the life of Jesus, and noticed poverty all over it:

> Look at the parameters of this mirror, that is the poverty of Him Who was placed in a manger and wrapped in swaddling clothes. O marvelous humility, O astonishing poverty! The King of the angels, the Lord of heaven and earth, is laid in a manger! Then, at the surface of the mirror, dwell on the holy humility, the blessed poverty, the untold labors and burdens which He endured for the redemption of all mankind. Then, in the depths of the same mirror, contemplate the ineffable charity which led Him to suffer on the wood of the Cross and die thereon the most shameful kind of death. Therefore, that Mirror, suspended on the wood of the Cross, urged those who passed by to consider, saying: 'All you who pass by the way, look and see if there is any suffering like My suffering!'[20]

From the poverty of the child resting in an animal's feeding trough, through the labour and burdens of life in Nazareth and Galilee, to the shame and pain of death: the whole life of Jesus, the Mirror, reflects back to Clare her own face. In living the way she and her sisters live, like Francis and his brothers, she is mirroring the Mirror who is Jesus, God-with-us. She describes her own experience in relationship with Francis in terms that sound very close to her description of the life of Jesus, including poverty, work, suffering and shame:

> The Blessed Father saw that we had no fear of poverty, hard work, suffering, shame, or the contempt of the world, but that, instead, we regarded such things as great delights, moved by compassion he wrote for us a form of life.[21]

Her firm intention to remain, with her sisters, in 'holy poverty' created real difficulties for her and her sisters for many years. She was especially concerned that church authorities would not honour their intention to live without any fixed source of income. Such a life *sine proprio* made little sense to well-intentioned benefactors. They failed to grasp that the choice to live without possessing anything lay at the heart of Clare's spirituality, her way into the mystery of Christ.

When the Fourth Lateran Council (1215) prohibited the approval of any new religious rules, the sisters at San Damiano were given the Rule of St Benedict as the juridical basis for their common life. This Rule made Benedict, not Francis, their founder, something Clare would not accept. The Benedictine Rule also allowed for ownership of property in common. It would be forty years later, as Clare lay dying, that her own Rule for the sisters would be approved. To affirm the distinctive character of her community's way of life, during the years following the Council's decision she requested and received from the Pope, Innocent III, a highly unusual 'privilege' to mark that difference. A 'privilege' was a special law or an exemption from a general law, usually given to grant some favour or advantage to the one making the petition. What Clare requested was the 'favour' of not accepting any favours.

> Innocent, Bishop, Servant of the servants of God, to his beloved daughters in Christ, Clare and the other servants of Christ of the Church of San Damiano in Assisi, professing the regular life, both those in the present, as well as those in the future for ever:

> As is evident, you have renounced the desire for all temporal things, desiring to dedicate yourselves to the Lord alone. Because of this, since you have sold all things and given them to the poor, you propose not to have any possessions whatsoever, clinging in all things to the footprints of Him, the Way, the Truth and the Life, Who, for your sake, was made poor ... Therefore, we confirm with our apostolic authority, as you requested, your proposal of most high poverty granting you by the authority of this letter that no one can compel you to receive possessions.[22]

Having just received the Benedictine Rule, which allows for ownership of property by the monastic community, Clare and her sisters immediately asked for an exception, that they would not have to possess anything, either individually or as a community. This was unheard-of in the Church at that time. Women's communities needed to receive dowries from women entering the community, often in the form of agricultural land that could be leased out to tenant farmers to provide revenue. And monasteries could expect to receive bequests from benefactors, either land or the income from rental properties, or a percentage of the income from a mill or vineyard. It was customary for church authorities to demand a certain level of predictable revenue for each community, depending on the number of women belonging to it. Clare asked specifically to be exempted from receiving any property whatsoever, out of a firm intention to follow the poverty of Christ. And we should remember that she requested this radical innovation in church policy only three years after starting the community at San Damiano, at the age of twenty-two!

As a contemporary author explains it, the official papal document issued by Innocent III is remarkable, and it must have seemed a kind of juridical 'monster' to canon lawyers of Clare's day:

> The *Privilege* recalls the beginnings of the community when several young women, who ardently desired to dedicate their entire lives to the Lord, chose to sell their goods

and to distribute the proceeds to the poor. They proposed to live with no possessions, following in the footprints of the poor Christ. The really remarkable aspect of the document arises from the fact that it considers poverty as a juridical value. What we have here is a short juridical *monstrum* which must have been a considerable surprise to the thirteen-century experts in canon law. The *Privilege of Poverty* (*Privilegium paupertatis*) is in fact the *privilege of living without any privileges*. It is a privilege which guarantees a life with no guarantees. It is a privilege given directly by the pope, the highest authority in the Church, to a young laywoman who had made her profession of religious life into the hands of an uneducated layman.[23]

It would take the rest of Clare's life for her to convince a pope to extend this recognition of the 'differentness' of the way of life practised in the women's community at San Damiano. She was quite literally on her deathbed when she received that long-awaited, official approval of their unique way of life. On 9 August 1253, just two days before she died, Pope Innocent IV signed the official approval of Clare's Rule, confirming the way of life of the San Damiano community.

At the end of her life, after calling together all her sisters, she entrusted the *Privilege of Poverty* to them. Her great desire had been to have had the Rule of the Order confirmed with a papal seal and then, on the following day, to die. It all happened just as she had wanted. She learned that a brother had come with letters bearing the papal bull. She reverently took them, even though she was very close to death, and she pressed that seal to her mouth in order to kiss it.[24]

Clare's tenacity in clinging to this privilege is rooted in her conviction of the importance of poverty to Jesus, exemplified for her also in the way Francis and his brothers lived.

The Son of God never wished to abandon this holy poverty while he lived in the world, and our most blessed Father

Francis, following His footprints, never departed, either
in example or teaching, from this holy poverty which he
had chosen for himself and for his brothers.[25]

Clare, like Francis, did not choose poverty for philosophical
reasons, nor for practical ones, as a choice making her life
more productive or efficient. And neither of them speak about
this poverty as a response to the affluence of Church or society
in their day, though it was undoubtedly seen by others in
that way. The focus of their attention was God's overwhelming
generosity and love, expressed in the free choice of the Son to
embrace poverty in becoming a creature. The two disciples
from Assisi embraced poverty because it was embraced by
their Beloved.

POVERTY, SPIRITUALITY AND POLEMIC: THE SPIRITUALS

In his time as Minister General of the Order, Bonaventure
confronted a reform movement whose members were known
as 'Spiritual' Franciscans. Their name derives from a phrase
in the Rule which speaks of brothers who are seeking 'to
observe the Rule spiritually'. There Francis is talking about
obedience to those in authority ('ministers') and possible con-
flicts of conscience. Here is the important passage:

> Therefore I strictly command them to obey their ministers
> in all those things which they have promised the Lord to
> observe and which are not against [their] conscience and
> our Rule. And wherever there are brothers who know
> and realize that they cannot observe the Rule spiritually,
> it is their duty and right to go to the minister for help.[26]

As popes and General Chapters interpreted the Rule over the
years, certain exceptions were allowed in the practice of
poverty to encourage expanded opportunities for study and
various forms of stable ministry, especially in cities. With
larger communities and growing libraries, these 'new' types of

Franciscan houses disturbed the consciences of some friars, who felt unable 'to observe the Rule spiritually', and when they appealed to their ministers for help, they often received rebuke instead. They wanted the Order to return to smaller, contemplative groups of brothers living in hermitages, supporting themselves by manual labour and begging. Many of the Spirituals in fact lived in the hermitages of southern France and central Italy.

Meditating on the prophecies of Joachim of Fiore, many Franciscans, including Bonaventure, saw Francis as a prophetic figure, announcing the coming of a 'New Age' of the Spirit, one in which the Church would be renewed and reformed, and in which the Franciscan Order would play a pivotal role. Some Spirituals took this meditation a step further, promoting a dramatic, apocalyptic spirituality, in which their own sufferings at the hands of superiors in the Order and the Church only confirmed their special role as the 'elect' awaiting the dawning of a new spiritual age (and their enemies were then easily labelled as the 'Antichrist'). An outstanding example of this approach is the 'History of the Seven Tribulations of the Order of Minors', written by the leader of Italian Spirituals, Angelo Clareno (d. 1337).[27]

UBERTINO DA CASALE

A friar who was profoundly affected by the teaching of Angela of Foligno, Ubertino (d. 1330s) had been a student of Peter John Olivi (d. 1298), one of the great teachers of the Spirituals. Olivi and Ubertino emphasised poverty as essential to Christian perfection and, with other Spirituals, admired the apocalyptic spirituality of Joachim of Fiore.

In the Introduction to his work *Sanctitas vestra* ('Your Holiness'), Ubertino raises up what the Spirituals considered the fundamentals of the Franciscan way of living the gospel, proposing especially the example of their life as one of the seven fundamental qualities of the tradition. That life is lived in highest and hence pacific poverty; in most innocent simplicity, and thereby it eschews all subtlety and cunning; in spotless purity, hence set apart from the din of the world; in deep humility, whereby it avoids superiority, and anything inimical to respect for the hierarchy; in assiduous prayer and work, defence against distraction, idleness, greed and worldliness; in perfect charity, defence against mutual persecution and hatred; in being an example to others, and hence avoiding offence to the faint-hearted and the laity.[28]

But the 'highest and hence pacific poverty' of the Spirituals seemed dangerously close to views about the poverty of Christ that seemed heretical. Ubertino himself received his own punishment for his views: exiled to the hermitage at La Verna, Ubertino wrote his masterwork, the *Arbor vitae crucifixae Iesu* ('The Tree of Life of Jesus Crucified').[29] In the context of exile, under the censure of church authorities, Ubertino turned to meditation on the cross, not as a symbol only of suffering, but as a life-giving tree.

In an extended allegory, the *Arbor vitae* compares the life, suffering and death of Jesus to the roots, the trunk, branches and fruit of the Tree of Life. It also contains moving meditations on the inner life of Jesus, his suffering prompted by love, and that love itself as the moving force of salvation. Following Joachim, Ubertino predicted that the unfaithful and 'carnal' Church of his day would soon return to this life-giving Tree, after passing through the end of the sixth 'state' of salvation history. Francis inaugurated this era, one of spiritual renewal, and it continued in the work of his true followers, those who embrace Lady Poverty (that is, the Spiritual Franciscans). One of the visions of the Book of Revelation provided Ubertino with his point of reference: 'Then I saw another angel ascend from the rising of the sun, with the seal of the living God' (Revelation 7:2):

Let us now return to the perfection of Francis, declared to be the Angel of the Sixth Seal, not only by external witnesses but also by his most perfect life. He ascends from the rising of the sun: always rising from virtue to virtue of Christ's mortal life in his holy way of living, he modelled himself on the life of Christ. And he had preeminently the sign of the living God: because of the merit of his life he was found uniquely worthy to bear truly in his body the signs of the wounds of the Crucified. He shone uniquely with the life of Christ: as is clear from his observance of the Gospel; in crucifixion, profound humility, extreme poverty, burning charity, desire for our salvation, the suffering of the cross, and merciful condescension and compassion for sinners and the suffering.[30]

In the Book of Revelation, this angel (not identified as the 'sixth') calls for marking the elect with the sign of salvation (Revelation 7:3–8). But the 'sixth angel' blows his trumpet to unleash plagues that kill a third of humankind (Revelation 9:13–19), a prediction of the punishments to be inflicted on those who rejected salvation (thus a warning to Ubertino's opponents).

The *Arbor vitae*, with its fulminations against the Antichrist in the Church, also reflects the polemics of the time, especially the struggle between the Spirituals and Pope Boniface VIII. Other popes (Benedict XI, Clement V and John XXII) turned the forces of the Inquisition against these radical Franciscans. The movement met its own apocalypse in the person of John XXII. After arrests and excommunications, the last four Spirituals who refused to submit were burned alive in the market-square of Marseilles on 7 May 1318.

By the middle of the fourteenth century, the meaning of poverty in the Franciscan tradition had changed dramatically. From the desire to live *sine proprio* in Francis and Clare, the Spirituals transformed it into an apocalyptic sign, charged with notions of the impending upheaval of a corrupt and wealthy church establishment.

Despite the excesses of some of the Spirituals, we are beginning to see today the important service to the Franciscan tradition performed by these 'revolutionaries of the Spirit'. They remained familiar with the broad corpus of Francis' own writings, and kept alive valuable oral and written traditions about the early years of the Franciscan movement. Some of these traditions are reflected (and coloured by the Spirituals' prejudices) in works like *The Mirror of Perfection* and the *Fioretti*, 'The Little Flowers of Saint Francis'. And their relentless emphasis on the early style of life in hermitages helped to shape revivals of the practice of poverty and contemplation for centuries. These revivals included the Observant movement in the fifteenth century; and the 'houses of recollection', 'retiros' and the Capuchin reform in the sixteenth century. These groups in turn were the living environment for important Franciscan mystics and spiritual writers, and for the development of forms of popular devotions, as well as systems of prayer, meditation and contemplation.

4. 'THE LORD LED ME AMONG THEM'

Francis uses the word 'sweetness' for God: 'You are all our sweetness'; God is 'delectable and sweet'.[1] In the *Testament*, Francis talks about his first taste of this sweetness, a savouring of the presence of God:

> While I was in sin, it seemed very bitter to me to see lepers. The Lord led me among them and I showed mercy to them. And when I left them that which seemed bitter to me was changed into sweetness of soul and body.[2]

Arnaldo Fortini, the former mayor of Assisi, assembled dramatic evidence from city archives to document the life of people with leprosy during Francis' lifetime. In those documents we learn that town officials, accompanied by a priest, went door to door at regular intervals to examine people of the town for signs of the disease. White blotches on the skin served as evidence that a person was infected. At that moment a whole life ended: the *lebbroso* had to leave family and home, possessions and security, to be 'enclosed' in the hospital of San Lazzaro dell'Arce, the leprosarium outside the town, on the plain below, near the old chapel of the Porziuncola. Dedicated to Saint Lazarus, this hospital's name evoked both Lazarus, whom Jesus raised from the dead (John 11) and Lazarus 'the poor man', 'full of sores' who wanted to eat the scraps that fell from the rich man's table (Luke 16:19–31).

Men and women with the infection, the *infetti* and *infette*, of every age and social rank, walked in a procession resembling a funeral cortège to their 'resting place' in the valley. The priest celebrated for them a type of funeral for the living in the hospital's chapel, sprinkling them with dirt from the adjacent cemetery. He declared them 'dead to the world' while promising that God would be merciful to them, the Church would pray for them, and the charity of townspeople would support them (their properties were confiscated by the town and used as an endowment to support the hospital).

They had to wear a distinctive habit of ash-coloured cloth, and warn others of their presence by sounding a wooden clapper like the one used in churches on Good Friday to replace the sound of bells. They could never touch food that was not placed in their own bowl; they could not draw water themselves from streams, wells or fountains; they could not even speak to others unless they first placed themselves down-wind from them. So great was the fear of contagion that a person with leprosy, discovered within the city walls after curfew had sounded, could be killed on the spot with impunity.[3]

FRANCIS' EXPERIENCE OF GOD AMONG LEPERS

'When I left them, that which seemed bitter to me was changed into sweetness of soul and body': Francis was recalling at the end of his life events of twenty years earlier. He uses a word for God's presence, 'sweetness', to describe being among the lepers and working for them. Why would he speak in this way? Francis experienced among them characteristics of God. In Jesus God gives up all 'property', even divine status, relying on alms and the care of others: in his birth among the poor, his life and travel among people considered of no account, in his suffering and dying, naked and shunned, even by close friends and relatives. The people with leprosy were 'brother Christians', special people, 'bearing the meaning' of who God is: the humble, poor Lover. This helps us to understand Francis' words:

> [The brothers] must rejoice when they live among people [who are considered to be] of little worth and who are looked down upon, among the poor and the powerless, the

> sick and the lepers, and the beggars by the wayside . . .
> [The Lord Jesus Christ] was a poor man and a transient
> and lived on alms, He and the Blessed Virgin and His
> disciples.[4]

To be among such people is to be in the community of Jesus,
and among those by the wayside, those who had contracted
leprosy were especially dear to him.

Service to the lepers was the first work of the brothers and
leper houses provided a home for the friars. When he was
travelling, Francis would visit lepers along the way: 'He
was riding on an ass when he had to pass through Borgo San
Sepolcro . . . he wanted to rest at a certain house of lepers.'[5]

FOLLOWING THE FOOTSTEPS OF JESUS

In his care for people with Hansen's disease, Francis was following that example of Jesus that he knew from the gospel.
Jesus calls others, after his wilderness retreat, to conversion,
to repent, to change their lives. To show the effects of this
turning to God Jesus does something specific: he heals people
who are suffering from disease, both physical disease and sick-
ness of spirit (Matthew 4:23–4). Later in the Gospel, Matthew
says, 'When he came down from the mountain, great crowds
followed him, and a leper came to him,' whom Jesus healed
(Matthew 8:1–3).

The special role of people with leprosy appears in the exceptions that Francis makes where they are concerned, even in
the Rule. Despite his strict prohibitions about receiving money,
he makes special provisions for one group of people: the
brothers 'may accept money for urgent needs of the lepers'.[6]
He places in his list of the 'companions of Jesus' the sick,
those who beg, and lepers, including them with the Lord Jesus
Christ, the Virgin Mary, and the disciples among those who live
by alms. The brothers should 'rejoice' to be in their company.

In his own writings Francis does not speak of the voice from
the crucifix at San Damiano telling him to 'rebuild the church'.

He never refers to the marks on his body (the stigmata), which others associated with his profound compassion for the sufferings of Christ. Rather Francis speaks about people with leprosy as the context for his conversion to the gospel way of life, the practical experience of 'being with' them, and serving them. Here he found the suffering members of Christ's Body, and beginning with this experience he participated in the passion of Christ.

Penitents served in the leper hospital of Assisi already, so Francis 'did mercy' most likely in the midst of other brother and sister penitents who had taken on this service at the risk of contracting the disease themselves (a widespread fear at the time). To go 'among the lepers' meant exposing himself to risk, for the sake of others considered 'dead to the world'. There may even be reasons to suggest that Francis' multiple illnesses in later life may have derived from infection with the tubercular form of Hansen's disease. And during his lifetime, or shortly thereafter, a place for the brothers who contracted the disease was established at San Lazzaro del Valloncello, outside Assisi.[7]

LEPROSY IN EARLY FRANCISCAN DOCUMENTS

In the first *Life* of Francis, Thomas of Celano recounts how Francis went 'to be among the lepers, and lived with them', 'serving their every need out of the love of God'. He washed them, dressed their sores, 'as he himself says in his Testament'.[8] To return to his first fervour, even at the end of his life he wanted to return among the lepers.[9]

In the second collection of stories assembled by Thomas, some twenty years later, the emphasis has shifted to the miraculous. Rather than emphasising the physical labour of working in a leper hospital, Thomas recounts the story of a single leper whom Francis meets on the plain below Assisi. This is the famous scene of Francis as he kisses the leper. After he has given him some money, along with a kiss, Francis mounts his horse. Looking around ('though the plain lay open on every side') he could see no sign of the leper.[10]

We may note here that care for people with Hansen's disease was no longer a primary work of the brothers by the 1240s, when Thomas composed his second text. This may help us to understand the emphasis on a miraculous deed, rather than the practical, day-to-day contact with leprosy that characterised the early days of the movement.

By the 1260s, when Bonaventure composed his *Major Life* of Francis, the importance of caring for people with leprosy is further diminished. In describing the same scene, that of Francis' encounter with the disappearing leper, Bonaventure casts the whole account in terms of an exercise in virtue. In order to fulfil his desire for perfection, and to become a 'soldier of Christ' (2 Timothy 2:3), Francis had first to 'conquer himself'. For this reason, he kisses the leper after giving him money, after which he could see the leper nowhere.[11]

Memories of the 'good old days' of the early Franciscan movement are presented in the *Legend of Perugia*. This text, also called the *Assisi Compilation*, seems intent to offer an alternative to Bonaventure's 'official' life of the founder. And here the role of the lepers in the daily, lived experience of spirituality and contemplation among the brothers has an outstanding importance. As it describes life at the Porziuncola, which Francis considered as a place for the contemplative life, people with leprosy seem to be quite at home. There, Brother James 'sometimes brought several lepers to the church of St Mary' from the leper hospital, since 'in those days the brothers lived in leper-hospitals'.[12] These 'Brother Christians' (Francis' name for people with the disease) participated in the life of Francis and the brothers in this prototype of the Franciscan hermitages: the brothers 'preserved its holiness by praying there continually night and day and by observing silence there'.[13] The tradition of Franciscan contemplation began in this precise historical context, outside the urban centre, on the margins of society, among the despised and feared minority of 'Brother' and 'Sister Christians'.

Jordan of Giano, in his *Chronicle* composed in the 1260s, makes frequent reference to the importance of lepers in the early fraternity. Their homes were places for meetings and lodging for the brothers. The identification of Francis' followers with the lepers even went to what Jordan considered an extreme. He makes reference to the founding of a religious community for people with leprosy, while Francis was in the Middle East:

> Brother John Conpella, after he had gathered together a large crowd of lepers, both men and women, withdrew from the Order and wanted to be the founder of a new Order. He wrote a Rule and presented himself with his followers before the Holy See to have it confirmed.[14]

Brother Jordan's objection to Brother John's initiative does not seem to arise from any question about sharing in the lives of lepers, but rather from John's decision to leave the Order of the brothers and seek 'letters from the Roman Curia', which Francis explicitly forbade in his *Testament*.[15]

In 1223 or 1224, the first Chapter meeting of the brothers in Germany was held, 'on the feast of the Nativity of the Blessed Virgin Mary at Speyer at the leprosarium outside the walls'.[16] Brother Jordan himself travelled with a group of brothers to begin a Franciscan settlement at Erfurt. They arrived in November, and 'since it was winter and not a time for building', the brothers stayed 'in the house of a priest who was in charge of the lepers outside the walls'.[17]

As older brothers like Jordan looked back to the early years of their fraternity they remembered clearly that the context for much of their early experience of the origins of the Franciscan tradition was that of communities of people with leprosy. The gatherings of the brothers, their places of prayer, their living quarters were with the lepers, their 'Brother Christians'. But this was also a kind of nostalgia, looking back, in Jordan's case, to a period forty years earlier. As the brothers exchanged working and living in leper hospices for new types of ministry in larger urban churches, the early experience gradually became an example of spiritual heroism to be admired, but not necessarily imitated.

The care for those suffering from leprosy was not, however, forgotten. Though the Lesser Brothers had embarked on new styles of life and ministry, the Brothers and Sisters of Penance expanded their role of caring for the sick in hospitals for lepers and others. Toward the close of the thirteenth century these Franciscan penitents, following the example of Francis himself, made their service of the sick a fundamental expression of Franciscan spirituality, seeing in their suffering the presence of Christ.

ANGELA AND THE EUCHARIST OF LEPROSY

One of the most striking accounts of this spirituality comes to us from the autobiographical *Memorial* of Angela of Foligno. Angela recounts an experience on Holy Thursday, probably in 1292, that takes place at a hospital, probably the leprosarium of San Lazzaro di Corsiano, outside the walls of Foligno. The whole incident, in Angela's vivid language, is worth reproducing here:

> On Maundy Thursday, I suggested to my companion that we go out to find Christ: 'Let's go,' I told her, 'to the hospital and perhaps we will be able to find Christ there among the poor, the suffering, and the afflicted.' We brought with us all the head veils that we could carry, for we had nothing else. We told Giliola, the servant at that hospital, to sell them and from the sale to buy some food for those in the hospital to eat. And, although initially she strongly resisted our request, and said we were trying to shame her, nonetheless, because of our repeated insistence, she went ahead and sold our small head veils and from the sale bought some fish. We had also brought with us all the bread which had been given to us to live on.
>
> And after we had distributed all that we had, we washed the feet of the women and the hands of the men, and

especially those of one of the lepers which were festering and in an advanced stage of decomposition. Then we drank the very water with which we had washed him. And the drink was so sweet that, all the way home, we tasted its sweetness and it was as if we had received Holy Communion. As a small scale of the leper's sores was stuck in my throat, I tried to swallow it. My conscience would not let me spit it out, just as if I had received Holy Communion.[18]

This account, though it may seem shocking, puts into action the profound intuition expressed in Francis' *Testament*, to which the text may allude: the 'bitter' becomes 'sweet', a recognition of the presence of God.

The spread of Hansen's disease decreased in the fourteenth century, only to be replaced by the scourge of plagues. Franciscan men and women shifted their attention to the victims of these new epidemics. It would be the great merit of the Brothers and Sisters of Penance in succeeding centuries to keep alive that tradition of service to the sick as an integral part of the Franciscan tradition, through the establishment of hospitals and communities to serve them, the origin of many communities of the Third Order Regular Franciscans.[19]

LEPROSY AND LIBERATION

In the context of Latin American theologies of liberation, Leonardo Boff has pointed to a way of recovering the importance of Francis' 'com-passion' toward lepers. His book, *Saint Francis: A Model for Human Liberation*[20] carries a subtitle, 'a reading beginning with the poor', suggesting a new way to read the story of Francis in today's context of global impoverishment.

For Boff, Francis not only lives 'with' the poor or 'for' them, he lives 'as' the poor, among those with leprosy, and those who are left 'on the side of the road' in his day. His great gift of 'com-passion', the capacity to share their suffering, requires tenderness and strength, both of which he finds in the passion of God, in Christ.[21]

A serious rereading of the Franciscan sources from the point of view of the poor helps to restore to its original, central place the 'disappeared' disease that so profoundly marked the origins of Franciscan spirituality. To recover that memory today would mean broadening its meaning beyond Hansen's disease, now a treatable illness, though still a serious threat in many countries. In our own time Human Immuno-deficiency Virus and Auto-Immune Deficiency Syndrome have compromised the health and caused the death of people around the globe. Like Hansen's disease in the thirteenth century, these conditions have provoked in the twentieth century attitudes of panic and condemnation. But some Franciscans have also found among our brothers and sisters living with HIV and AIDS the 'sweetness' that Francis always regarded as the irrefutable sign of the presence of God.

5. 'THE SPIRIT OF PRAYER AND HOLY DEVOTION'

Francis and his companions 'followed the footsteps' of Jesus also by integrating prayer with preaching, work and travel. They set aside time daily for liturgical prayer and took opportunities for prayer alone, in hermitages, apart from the surrounding society and towns. In this chapter we will examine some of those activities considered the 'spiritual practices' of the Franciscan tradition.

But we should use that term cautiously, because it suggests a dichotomy between the 'material' side of that tradition (work, travel, relationships) and the 'spiritual' (identified with practices of prayer or meditation). Hopefully, at this point in our treatment of the Franciscan tradition, such a division seems artificial, as it should. Prayer, contemplation, life in the hermitage: these are a part, but only a part, of the 'full gospel' spirituality of Francis, Clare and their followers.

Francis is not notable in the history of spirituality for developing or teaching techniques of prayer or meditation. His preferred phrases describe a basic attitude toward prayer as an underlying condition of life: to have 'the spirit of prayer and holy devotion'; to desire 'the spirit of the Lord and his holy operation'.[1] Preserving this spirit was to take precedence over every kind of work, and every other concern, including the study of theology.[2] It was not identical with practices of prayer, since some say 'many prayers' but easily grow angry when criticised by others: they are not truly 'poor in spirit', the condition for all genuine prayer.[3]

PRAYING TOGETHER

When we attempt to reconstruct the early Franciscan prayer schedule for the day and the whole year, we can see how 'the spirit of prayer' expressed itself in practice. The early Franciscan community made no systematic attempt to separate contemplative prayer from vocal prayer, nor private prayer from common prayer. These were woven together in a fabric of prayer and devotion throughout the brothers' daily and yearly schedule. Prayer in common filled a large part of that schedule.

They celebrated the Liturgy of the Hours each day. In the Rule, the celebration of the Office is required for all the brothers, whether cleric or lay. Those who could read Latin, the cleric brothers, were to use the breviary; those who could not, the lay brothers, were to pray the 'Our Father' while the clerics recited the psalms.[4] In the *Rule for Hermitages*, Francis advises that the hours of the Office are to be celebrated in this way: Compline, after sunset; Matins (probably including Lauds, and usually celebrated very early in the morning); then the daytime offices of Prime, Terce, Sext, None and Vespers 'at the proper time'.[5] This celebration of the Office would have required at least several hours each day. The Office was probably celebrated with some form of chant, since Francis emphasised that all should pay more attention to their praying than their melody (perhaps then as now, not all could keep in tune). But the emphasis here is on sincerity of heart ('the spirit of prayer') along with liturgical simplicity: they used the breviary, the shorter, portable Office book used by the staff of the Roman Curia, not the multi-volume monastic Office with its more complex form of chant. Celano notes that even when travelling Francis would stop at the various times for prayer to recite the Hours with his travelling companions. He always wanted to have another 'cleric' with him, a brother who could read, so that they could celebrate the Office together. The brothers also prayed an 'Office of the Passion', composed by Francis, to complement the breviary Office.[6] Other prayers that Francis composed for the brothers would also have been regularly included, for example, 'The Praises' said before the Office: 'You are good, all good, the highest good, the only good.'[7]

At first glance it may appear odd that nowhere in this detailed schedule of prayer does Francis mention the eucharistic liturgy. This is understandable if we consider that the early fraternity of Lesser Brothers did not at first include priests, only brothers, distinguished as 'cleric' and 'lay' in regard to their reading ability. To participate in the Mass, they would have gone to the nearest church or monastery. Thomas of Celano indicates that Francis himself wished to attend Mass every day and received Communion frequently, at a time when this was uncommon.[8]

In the later years of Francis' life the fraternity did have brothers who were priests, Anthony of Padua, for example. Francis wrote his *Letter to the Entire Order* in part to encourage all his 'brother priests' to celebrate the Mass with devotion. He stipulated that only one Mass be celebrated each day in the places where the brothers lived: if several priests were present, one should celebrate and the others participate with the rest of the brothers.[9]

The picture that emerges from what we know about the practice of daily prayer among Francis and his brothers indicates that 'the spirit of prayer and holy devotion' was expressed through dedicating significant time each day to liturgical prayer in common, both in the Office and the Eucharist. This liturgical prayer, however, was only a part of a more comprehensive life of prayer, which included times for prayer alone, in solitude, and whole seasons spent in hermitages, where Francis and his brothers lived an innovative form of contemplative life.

PRAYING ALONE

Francis and the brothers made time for what we would call private prayer (the sources usually prefer the gospel expression, 'praying in secret'). Thomas of Celano describes

some of these times in his second *Life* of Francis.[10] He mentions
that Francis would frequently pray alone during the night,
making a lot of noise going to sleep and then getting up very
quietly to pray without waking the brothers (obviously
someone must not have been fooled by this and observed him).
What happened when Francis prayed alone? Again, we must
rely on the observations of indiscreet observers. Celano says
that sometimes he would meditate within himself 'without
moving his lips', while at other times he would talk out loud
to the Lord. Sometimes he made noises, sighing and weeping,
and striking his breast. This experience seems to have been
very intense: companions noted that Francis seemed changed
in appearance, as if 'glowing' or 'melting', when he returned
from praying by himself. He was 'touched' by God in some
way during these encounters. To his embarrassment, these
'touches' also happened at times when he was with other
people. Then he would pull his mantle around him 'to make a
cell', or would at least cover his face with his sleeve so that
others could not observe what was happening to him when he
was 'caught up out of himself'.

By himself, in the company of other people, travelling or
staying with the brothers, during the daytime and at night,
Francis made the 'spirit of prayer and holy devotion' the organising principle of his daily schedule. But he also observed
special seasons of prayer, periods of solitude and contemplation.

SEASONS OF SOLITUDE

According to his companion, Brother Leo, Francis observed a
'Lent' on the mountain of La Verna to honour St Michael in
1224.[11] Lents like that of St Michael established a regular
rhythm, an annual schedule of special times for fasting, prayer
and solitude: five of them are mentioned in early sources.
First, and most important, is the 'Great Lent', observed in
Spring with prayer and fasting for forty days before Easter.
Then there is the late Autumn Lent preparing for Christmas,

beginning after the Feast of All Saints, 1 November. These two Lents were observed by all the brothers, as written in their *Rule*.[12] There was also a Winter Lent, recommended but not required of the brothers, after the Epiphany, 6 January, until the beginning of the Great Lent on Ash Wednesday in the Spring. Francis observed a Lent in Summer, from the feast of Sts Peter and Paul, 29 June, until the Assumption, 15 August. Finally, the Lent of St Michael mentioned above began after the Assumption and ended on 29 September.[13]

We have indications from the sources of how Francis observed these Lents: in fasting, solitude and prayer. One Great Lent Francis spent on an island in Lake Trasimene, near Perugia. A fisherman rowed him out to the island, and Francis took with him just a little bread, and asked to be brought back to shore at the conclusion of Lent. It was at the end of a Lent preparing for Christmas that Francis arranged for the display of the living nativity scene at Greccio. During the Lent of St Michael at La Verna, he was accompanied by Brother Leo, with whom he prayed the Office, while spending most of the time in prayer alone. If these are indicative of his usual practice each year, Francis would spend probably three and perhaps five periods of about forty days each in relative seclusion, dedicating himself to prayer in solitude, usually with one of the brothers. This would total four months to seven months a year in a secluded, contemplative way of life, frequently spent in the hermitages, a characteristic feature of early Franciscan spiritual practice.

THE HERMITAGE AND CONTEMPLATIVE LIFE

The early Franciscan hermitages were only one of many expressions of a renewed interest in forms of contemplative life in Francis' day. In the century before Francis, Cistercians, Camaldolese and Carthusians had championed the renewal of contemplative life within the monastic tradition. The Cistercians reduced the elaborate Office of other monasteries (like Cluny) to a simpler, briefer form; they emphasised silence, poverty and manual labour, striving for a more perfect observance of the Rule of St Benedict. St Bernard of Clairvaux, William of St Thierry and Isaac of Stella were among the early Cistercian authors whose writings on prayer and contemplation had an influence far beyond their own communities. Beginning in France, Cistercian monasteries covered western Europe in the early thirteenth century, with important centres in Italy.

The Carthusians, under St Bruno, pursued the ideal of a solitary, eremitical life lived in the context of a community of solitaries, like that of some of the early Desert Fathers. Within the Charterhouse (*Chartreuse*) each had his own cell in which to sleep, work, study and pray, and had a small, enclosed garden attached. The community prayed together three times a day; at other times each monk prayed in his own cell, where he also took his meals, except on Sundays and feast days when the community ate together. From their earliest home in the mountains of France, the Carthusians, including Bruno himself, also made new foundations in Italy.

The Camaldolese, beginning with St Romuald, had also combined a common life with the life of hermits, following the Benedictine Rule. At the hermitage, the *Sacro Eremo*, high in the mountains of north-central Italy, near Mount La Verna, the monks lived an eremitical life, living in separate cells where they could spend most of their time in solitude and prayer. Below the hermitage, other monks lived a cenobitic monastic life, a life in community, but always with the possibility of moving to the hermitage above for greater solitude.

But these monastic reform movements did not exhaust the enthusiasm of twelfth-century Christians for 'the life of the desert'. Many lay 'penitents' went seeking solitude in the mountains and forests of France, England and Italy during the twelfth century. They lived in the wilderness in austere, often beautiful, hermitage settings where they dedicated themselves to a life of prayer and penance, combined with manual labour and charitable care for the other 'social outcasts' who were condemned to live outside the towns of medieval Europe:

lepers, debtors and accused criminals. Some of these hermits lived in almost complete isolation, while others engaged in some preaching, wandering from place to place, frequently venerated as living saints, sometimes denounced by bishops and clergy as disturbers of the peace and heretics. Some, like Robert of Arbrissel in France, attracted numerous followers and founded what would become religious, eventually monastic, communities, including both men and women.[14]

To his fellow citizens in Assisi, the young Francis must have seemed another of these lay hermits. In the early days of his conversion Francis lived as a lay penitent, dressed in the typical clothing of a hermit, seeking solitary places for prayer, serving lepers, repairing ruined churches.

But he also had ample opportunity to know something of the monastic tradition. In his search for solitude, he could have visited the cells once inhabited by Byzantine monks (refugees from Islamic forces in the East) on the plateau of Mount Subasio above Assisi. He certainly had some contact with the monks of San Benedetto, the great Benedictine abbey on the mountain, who later allowed him to stay at their property of the Porziuncola. When Francis visited Rome, one of his supporters at the papal court was a Cistercian monk, Cardinal John of St Paul, and the influence of Cistercian tradition is noticeable in some of Francis' *Admonitions*.

Francis probably visited the ancient monastic settlement founded by St Benedict at Subiaco, between Assisi and Rome, where a striking portrait of 'brother Francis' without the halo of a saint (before his canonisation in 1228) was frescoed in the cave where Benedict used to spend time in solitary prayer. Later in his life, Francis used the mountain of La Verna, near Camaldoli, as a special place of prayer and solitude. An ancient tradition at Camaldoli holds that Francis was a guest at the *Sacro Eremo*, and one of the cells there bears his name.

Francis had some familiarity with important monastic and lay renewal movements proposing a renewal of a contemplative or eremitical life, frequently inspired by the example of the Desert Fathers in fourth-century Egypt. Yet he did not join one of the pre-existing groups. Thomas of Celano pictures him as even resisting the suggestion of his Cistercian supporter, John of St Paul, that he join these communities of 'monks or hermits'.[15] Always turning toward the life he read about in the Gospels, Francis would attempt to unite the eremitical life with the life of the travelling preacher of the Good News.

FRANCIS' CREATIVE BALANCE

Francis experienced a tension within himself about the direction of God's call for him, a creative tension between his desire for a life of contemplation and a life of preaching. He discussed this question with his first group of brothers, whether they should 'seek solitary places' or live 'among the people'. The decision was made, after prayer, to live 'for others', after the example of Christ who gave his life 'for all'.[16] But this did not mean abandoning the ideal of solitude, but integrating it with the demands of preaching and living among the people. In fact, Francis is portrayed as withdrawing for longer periods to the solitude of the hermitages during the later years of his life.

Francis wrote a special Rule 'for those who wish to live religiously in hermitages'.[17] This Hermits' Rule gives us some indications of the balance of the values of contemplation, work and fraternity in Francis' life, and probably offers a good picture of the kind of environment in which Francis spent many of his Lents. Three or four brothers stayed at the hermitage at any one time, with some taking care of the household chores while the others were free to dedicate themselves to longer periods of prayer. These two groups were identified, respectively, as the 'mothers', who had the role of Martha, and their 'sons', in the role of Mary. Each had a cell, probably a small hut, and there was some gathering place for prayer and meals. As explained above, the Hours of the Office were prayed at their proper time, beginning with the early morning rising for Matins (Vigils). The meals were prepared and presumably eaten in common, since the brothers were not to eat in their own cells. The 'mothers', besides the daily chores and preparing meals, met visitors and kept them from disturbing those who were praying, their 'sons'. The Minister (superior of the region) could come freely to visit the brothers, but other guests were not allowed inside. Every so often, 'as it seemed best to them', the sons took their turn being mothers, and the mothers became their sons. This Rule for the hermitages shows great flexibility and expresses little concern about details of when, where and how the brothers' life was organised. It focuses on the essentials: praying; taking care of necessary work; and keeping outside distractions to a reasonable minimum.

The hermitage of the Carceri on the side of Mount Subasio overlooking Assisi became famous after Francis' lifetime as a model of this style of life. Early descriptions of life at the Porziuncola, in the valley below Assisi, the centre of the Franciscan movement in Francis' day, as well as recent archaeological excavations, indicate that it may be one of the earliest of these hermitages: a little chapel for common prayer, with a group of small huts for the brothers arranged around it, one with a cooking hearth, the whole complex surrounded by some kind of hedge (the enclosure) and woods around that. Other places where Francis frequently spent time also seem to have been organised in this way: Fonte Colombo, Greccio, and La Verna are often referred to as hermitages, and to some degree all of these, along with the Carceri, have kept to this day a tradition of a more contemplative type of Franciscan life. In recent times, the type of contemplative life in the Franciscan hermitages, with their flexibility and simplicity, gained the admiration of the great promoter of modern eremitical and contemplative life, Thomas Merton, in his lovely essay on 'Franciscan Eremitism'.[18]

BONAVENTURE

In the generation following the deaths of the founders, Bonaventure made the greatest contribution to organising major themes and images of the Franciscan School into a coherent spiritual–theological system. After becoming a 'Master' of theology, he experienced at first hand the famous conflict between 'seculars and mendicants' at the university, a dispute about the legitimacy of the 'new' Orders (Franciscans and Dominicans) and their role in the Church. Along with his contemporary, Thomas Aquinas, he wrote in defence of the new Orders, particularly his own. He also has left us a large body of theological works, exegesis and homilies. Elected as Minister General of the Order, he wrote eloquently and decisively about the Franciscan way of life, its founder St Francis, and the spirituality he bequeathed to his followers. At the instruction of the Order's General Chapter he wrote his *Major Life* of Francis, which was later adopted as the 'official' account of the founder's life and intentions. A subsequent Chapter decreed the elimination of all earlier Lives, leaving his to dominate the landscape of Franciscan spirituality until the last century.

In addition to his *Major Life* of Francis, Bonaventure also wrote his work of mystical theology, *The Soul's Journey into God*, in which he uses the figure of Francis and the vision of the Seraph on La Verna as a guide to 'rapture in contemplation'. Over the centuries it has remained one of the classic texts of the Franciscan tradition. In this masterful summary of steps leading to union with God, Bonaventure begins by explicitly invoking the example of Francis as his inspiration.

> Following the example of our most blessed father Francis, I was seeking this peace with panting spirit . . . [A]bout the time of the thirty-third anniversary of the Saint's death [1259], under divine impulse I withdrew to Mount La Verna, seeking a place of quiet and desiring to find there peace of spirit. While I was there reflecting on various ways by which the soul ascends into God, there came to mind, among other things, the miracle which had occurred to blessed Francis in this very place: the vision of a winged Seraph in the form of the Crucified. While reflecting on this, I saw at once that this vision repre-

sented our father's rapture in contemplation and the road by which this rapture is reached.[19]

Bonaventure then maps this contemplative journey toward rapture. The movement of the journey begins outside ourselves with careful attention to the world of creatures surrounding us. This world of creatures already shows us something of God, though a shadowy resemblance. There is some light, but it is like the evening twilight in which we see dimly. The journey continues with attention directed inward, as we discover a clearer image of God impressed within ourselves, body, mind and soul. This light, Bonaventure says, is like the growing light of dawn, in which we see more clearly than at dusk. The journey then moves upward, toward contemplation of God as God is, searching for the true likeness of God. Eventually baffled by the mysterious, simultaneous presence of unity and trinity, Being and Truth, our intellectual understanding is enveloped in darkness, blinded by a light like that of the sun at midday. Now in darkness, unable to understand, we seem to have come to the end of our journey. But at this moment we meet, not with our intellect, but with our heart's affection, the true likeness of God, and the resolution of all the seeming contradictions in God. This is Jesus, crucified, burning with love, inflaming our hearts, though our understanding is darkened.

> [I]t now remains for our mind,
> by contemplating these things,
> to transcend and pass over not only this sense world
> but even itself.
> In this passing over,
> Christ is the way and the door;
> Christ is the ladder and the vehicle.[20]

And here Bonaventure again invokes the example of Francis himself as 'an example of perfect contemplation'. Through him, 'more by example than by word', God invites every truly spiritual person 'to this kind of passing over and spiritual ecstasy'.[21]

Here Bonaventure establishes an important principle of the Franciscan tradition of contemplation: its availability to every true seeker. Francis did not put into words a system or technique of contemplative prayer. What he did offer was himself, his 'example', which others can follow. And the high point of this example is Francis' loving rapture of contemplative union with the crucified Christ during his retreat on the mountain of La Verna shortly before his death. The way to follow Francis' example is not, ironically, the intellectual quest so dear to Bonaventure as a theologian. It is rather a journey, a passing over, at the level of the heart, not the mind:

> But if you wish to know how these things come about,
> ask grace not instruction,
> desire not understanding,
> the groaning of prayer not diligent reading...
> not light but the fire...
> This fire is God...
> and Christ enkindles it
> in the heat of his burning passion.[22]

GIOVANNI DE CAULIBUS

An important Franciscan writer whose work would influence later generations was the Tuscan Giovanni de Caulibus (d. c.1335). As Lázaro Iriarte noted in the Introduction of his translation of this work, the 'Meditations' are one of the most significant texts of medieval asceticism and mysticism. They are a profoundly personal, interior meditation on events in the life of Christ, in a style characteristic of the *Devotio moderna*.[23] The work was highly popular in its day, translated into many languages. Originally composed for a Poor Clare, it was later echoed in the *Vita Christi* of Ludolph of Saxony. In it we have a systematic approach to meditation on the Life of Christ, organised according to a weekly schedule, as in this 'Method to Use in Meditation on the Life of Christ'.

Now I want to give you a method to use when you preach or meditate on the preceding pages . . .

You should know that it is sufficient to meditate each time on a single episode or single word of which the Lord is protagonist, or which happened in his presence according to the Gospel account. You must make yourself present as if you were assisting at the event that is being described, remaining in simplicity, with the soul, as it were, naked.

. . . To meditate, choose a quiet hour . . . Divide the meditations in this way: start on Monday and go as far as the flight of Jesus into Egypt, and leave him there until Tuesday. Then, making the return trip with him, continue the meditation to the moment when Jesus opens the Book in the synagogue. Take up at that point on Wednesday, and go as far as the services offered to Jesus by Mary and Martha. Thursday take up the account again, up to the Passion. Friday and Saturday continue up to the moment of the Lord's resurrection. Finally, on Sunday, meditate on the whole account of the resurrection up to the end of the book.[24]

Here we have the kind of practical instruction in a method of 'discursive' prayer that would be a mainstay of various schools of spirituality in the following centuries. But the Franciscan tradition was also to move in other directions, particularly in Spain in the fifteenth and sixteenth centuries, with a renewed interest in the 'art of contemplation'.

THE GOLDEN AGE

The great flowering of Franciscan contemplative practice and reflection had its centre in Spain in the sixteenth century, the so-called 'Golden Age' of Spanish mysticism. The most familiar names from that period are probably those of the great Carmelite mystics and reformers, Teresa of Avila and John of the Cross. But there are also some very significant figures from the Franciscan tradition who contributed to that history as well.

The renewal of the Franciscan contemplative tradition in Spain and elsewhere grew out of a new form of the hermitage tradition of the Order. As mentioned earlier, in regard to the Spirituals, various reform movements after them turned back to the type of life modelled in Francis' Rule for brothers living in hermitages. In the latter part of the fourteenth century the movement called the 'Observance' grouped together communities of Lesser Brothers seeking a 'regular observance' of the Rule, with greater emphasis on poverty; emphasising the role of lay brothers (the head of the group was Paoluccio de'Trinci, a lay brother from Foligno); and a return to the life in hermitages, away from the larger urban friaries (*conventi*) and churches. It was the eventual dominance of this reform movement that led, in 1517, to the division of the Lesser Brothers (Friars Minor) into two distinct families: the Friars Minor Conventual and the Friars Minor of the Observance.

Another reform movement, with its centre in Spain, established *retiros*, contemplative Franciscan communities outside the large cities. These communities produced most of the great writers of Franciscan spirituality in Spain in the sixteenth century. As the movement spread to Italy, it inspired the foundation of other communities there. The Friars Minor Capuchin, founded in 1525, were originally called the Friars 'of Eremitical Life', because of their practice of the contemplative life in hermitages as a fundamental aspect of their Franciscan life. The Capuchins became another independent family of Friars Minor in 1619, and contributed greatly to the spreading of Franciscan spirituality during the Catholic Reformation, in the wake of the Council of Trent.

With this history in mind, let us turn to some of the authors from these new movements whose work contributed to the great revival of mysticism and contemplative prayer in Spain.

HENDRIK HERP

Little known today, but of great importance for understanding
Spanish mysticism of the 1500s, is the Flemish Franciscan
Hendrik Herp (d. 1477), also known as 'Harphius'. He was a
disciple of the mystic Jan Ruysbroeck, and belonged to the
Brothers of the Common Life in Delft, in the Netherlands.
(This community of Brothers also gave us the classic of Cath-
olic spirituality, *The Imitation of Christ*.) In 1450,
unexpectedly, he became a Franciscan, joining the Observant
Reform of the Friars Minor. Herp wrote several works on
Christian mysticism, including *Spieghel der volcomenheit* ('The
Mirror of Perfection') and a group of works assembled after
his death by his disciples, the *Theologia mystica*.[25]

The figure of Francis and the mystical writings of Bonaventure recur in his works, and he emphasises the affective (rather
than intellectual) approach to contemplation seen in the *Soul's
Journey*. Herp also expresses a great confidence that every
Christian can reach mystical union with God, and thus represents one of many Franciscan exponents of the
'democratisation of contemplation'.

> There follows the third and highest life, that called the
> transcendent contemplative life, represented by Mary
> Magdalene, who 'chose the better part' [Luke 10:27].
> According to the tradition of the Scriptures, human beings
> were created to be in the company of angels in glory ...
> The transcendent contemplative life occupies the highest
> rank in the divine illuminations. It therefore requires that
> a person climb many rungs of virtues, especially through
> true mortification. One must do all in one's power to
> prepare oneself beforehand, in a useful and sound way,
> to receive from God that supreme communication of the
> transcendent contemplative life. Sometimes people who
> are still in the life of proficients, or even beginners, receive
> this gift. Some [receive it] even in the first moment of
> their conversion, as happened to the Apostle St Paul. As

soon as he was converted he was taken up to the third heaven and saw God's essence as we will see God in glory [Acts 9:5; 2 Corinthians 12:2].[26]

His emphasis on a simple, direct and affective form of union with God aimed at making a simple form of contemplative prayer a common practice for lay men and women as well as members of religious communities. Early editions of the *Theologia mystica* were censured by Roman authorities for overly daring language about mystical union, but Herp's writings circulated widely and gained a place of primary importance within many Franciscan communities, even being required as regular weekly reading. They certainly made their way to Spain, where Herp's writings contributed to the development of Franciscan treatises on mysticism and the 'art' of contemplative prayer.

FRANCISCO DE OSUNA

Teresa of Avila's uncle, Don Pedro de Cepeda, gave her a book shortly after she had made her profession as a Carmelite nun. Though sick at the time, she read the book carefully and found that by following its guidance she began to have some of her early experiences of contemplative prayer.[27] The book was *The Third Spiritual Alphabet* (*Tercer abecedario espiritual*) by Francisco de Osuna (d. *c.*1540), a Spanish Franciscan.[28]

Osuna belonged to one of the reform movements within the Observant branch of the Franciscans that emphasised a return to the more contemplative style of life characteristic of the early Franciscan hermitages. The reformers established 'houses of recollection', beginning in Spain in the 1480s, and gradually spreading to other countries. In these communities friars practised a simple form of contemplative prayer called 'recollection'. This involved re-collecting the scattered pieces of our awareness, and focusing them in a simple, loving gaze toward God.

Francisco de Osuna's *Alphabet* served Teresa as an

important guide in her own practice of this prayer of recollection. In it Osuna articulated a technique suitable for people in many different circumstances, lay and religious. The consistent 'quieting' of the senses and intellectual reasoning during prayer leads to an inner silence, unencumbered by thinking. Then, in simple enjoyment of being with God, with the intellect at rest (here we hear an echo of Bonaventure), the heart is joined to God.

Today, when people speak of 'contemplation' or 'contemplative prayer', they often mean this type of quiet focusing of attention, and few would see anything objectionable in this practice. But these terms, in the context of the Counter-Reformation (or Catholic Reformation), aroused suspicions. Some practitioners of contemplative prayer claimed to be under the special guidance of the Holy Spirit. These *alumbrados*, 'the enlightened', also known as 'Quietists', rejected the mediation of ritual and sacrament, claiming to worship God 'in spirit and truth'. The Inquisition, fearful of these developments, vigorously prosecuted those suspected of this heresy. Not surprisingly, Teresa and others suffered unjustly as a result of these suspicions.

BERNARDINO DE LAREDO

Another story about Teresa of Avila demonstrates the lively interchange between the Carmelite and Franciscan traditions in sixteenth-century Spain. In the years following her experience of conversion in 1554 Teresa sought advice from lay men, priests and religious about her experiences of increasingly mystical forms of prayer. Unfortunately most of them showed apprehension, if not outright suspicion, toward Teresa's experiences, especially fears of 'illuminism'. Once again, it was a book from the Franciscan tradition that encouraged her, the *Ascent of Mount Sion (Subida del Monte Sion)* by the Franciscan lay brother and physician, Bernardino de Laredo (d. 1540).[29]

The following passage from Bernardino was the one that

served as an encouragement to Teresa as she confronted the difficult problem of 'thinking nothing', which some insisted was a trick of the devil. Instead, in the *Ascent*, she found this positive interpretation of the experience of quiet prayer.

> Let the beginning of your contemplation always be to lift your soul above all that is not God, in such a way that no thought has a place in you, no matter how good. This means that your contemplation, if it is to be quiet and perfect, does not need to busy itself with anything other than love. If this love is quiet in perfect contemplation, it does not need to think anything during that quietness, because the love of my God, in which my soul is occupied, is not something thinkable or intelligible that our understanding can comprehend; it is rather something desirable and lovable. There is no apprehending by the understanding, only affection, desires and the will.
>
> If the perfection of any contemplative consists in love of our Christ Jesus, in which thoughts are a hindrance, we must understand the meaning of the one who said that it is better in quiet contemplation to think nothing.[30]

In this major work, which he wrote in 1538 after completing two books on medicine and pharmacology, Bernardino follows a method similar to that of Bonaventure, describing a threefold process of the soul's drawing near to itself, entering within itself and soaring above itself. These processes he links with three forms of prayer: recollection, quiet and union.

In the time of recollection, the will becomes focused and we give up thinking or methodical reflection. Using our affective capacities, rather than intellectual ability, we enter the next phase, that of quiet, described in terms of a profound sleep, putting all our inner selves at rest. In a third phase, we experience sudden, brief moments of union with God purely as a gift, not because of any technique we use. In this seeming emptiness of 'thinking nothing', the heart is alive, leaping up toward God and, quoting Herp, he says 'the spirit in this space ceases to live unto itself, because it lives completely unto God'.[31]

BENET OF CANFIELD

Like the friars of the 'houses of recollection' the Capuchins promoted a revival of the Franciscan life of poverty and contemplation. Their early practices included two hours of 'mental prayer' daily. This form of prayer relied on meditations (on the life of Christ, passages from the Gospels) as an aid to reaching the goal of continuous contemplation.

The Capuchin friars exercised a predominant role in developing a new spirituality in seventeenth-century France. The art of spiritual direction, fundamental to this development, had been articulated in the previous century by Ignatius of Loyola (d. 1556). Among the French Capuchins spiritual direction found an outstanding spokesman in Benet or Benoît of Canfield (d. 1610), earlier known as William Fitch, an Englishman and a former Puritan.

In his *Rule of Perfection*[32] he made the characteristic Franciscan emphasis on the will, rather than the understanding, the centre of his teaching. True perfection consists in conforming our own will to the will of God in all things. At first glance such a method of spiritual practice may seem simply a matter of 'doing the right thing'. But Benet goes far beyond this conformity in external behaviour. He posits a real joining of the human will with the will of God in an unmediated and continuous union, with language that he borrows from Hendrik Herp.

Benet and the Capuchin spiritual writers of the seventeenth century could hardly have predicted the crisis that lay ahead for the tradition they popularised in France. In the wake of the Enlightenment, with the suppressions of religious communities preceding and following the French Revolution, the Franciscan tradition of contemplation went into eclipse. There were outstanding examples of heroism, even martyrs, in the following century, but the issues of survival far outweighted interest in producing texts on the contemplative life.

The seventh centenary of Francis' birth, in 1882, was a quiet affair. Only in the latter years of the nineteenth century, with the encouragement of Pope Leo XIII (d. 1903), himself a member of the Franciscan Third Order, did the Franciscan tradition begin to revive.

6. 'BY YOUR HOLY CROSS, YOU HAVE REDEEMED THE WORLD'

One prayer particularly dear to Francis was modelled on the liturgy for the Feast of the Exaltation of the Holy Cross (14 September):

> We adore you, Most Holy Lord Jesus Christ, in all Your churches in the whole world, and we bless You, because by Your holy cross You have redeemed the world.[1]

He included the text of this prayer in his *Testament*, recalling the 'great faith in churches' that the Lord had given him. His devotion to Christ's life-giving death on the cross is a central component of the *Office of the Passion* he composed for his own use and that of his brothers, and one which they recited daily, in addition to the Divine Office.

The Office is a collection of fifteen 'psalms' (actually a patchwork of verses from the Psalms and other scriptural texts), organising the hours to represent events of Christ's life, especially those of the Paschal Triduum, with special psalms for the seasons of Advent, Christmas, Easter and Ascension. Francis begins with Christ's suffering in the garden and his betrayal (Compline); the birth of Christ and his judgement by the Sanhedrin (Matins); the resurrection (Prime); the crucifixion (Terce); his carrying the cross (Sext); his glorious death (None); and the sharing of all creation in redemption (Vespers). The texts are selected in such a way that they become words spoken by Christ, and addressed to 'my holy Father'.[2]

What this Office reveals to us is Francis' deep identification with Jesus that allows him to speak from what we might call Jesus' point of view through the words of the psalms. Francis had set out very deliberately to follow an inspiration: 'to follow the footsteps of Our Lord Jesus Christ'. He did this in his actions, in showing mercy to the sick and the suffering, in his preaching repentance and conversion to the gospel, in the way he went away to deserted places to pray. All of these actions resembled externally events in the life of Jesus as told in the gospel accounts. But the Office of the Passion reveals a deeper dimension to this 'following': Francis has learned to 'put on the mind of Christ', and gives every indication of having changed internally, now seeing the world around him from a new point of view, that of the Lord he has been following.

A certain pedagogy is at work here, first in Francis, then practised by his followers, and one which will mark the Franciscan tradition in its later development as well. Francis does what he sees Jesus doing in the gospel, and from the repetition of the actions, gestures and words of Jesus, he comes gradually to think, react, speak and even pray 'as if' Jesus. This 'conformity to Christ' begins to characterise not only the gestures of Francis, but even his thoughts. In later Franciscan texts, this conformity of Francis to Christ finds it classic expression in meditations on the stigmata, leading to the portrayal of Francis as *alter Christus*, 'another Christ'.[3]

In Francis' prayers, we see him brimming over with gratitude to God for all good things. He is deeply aware of how little he can give back in return. He sings over and over again of the Love that has been revealed to him, a Love that moves him frequently to tears, especially when he thinks of the suffering that Love endures. He finds in his own suffering (his physical illness, anxiety for his brothers, inner darkness and doubt) a way of participating in the experience of Love. He discovers in this sharing of the life of Love a deep joy in the midst of suffering. That joy comes from 'being with' his Beloved.

THOMAS OF CELANO AND MYSTICISM OF THE PASSION

The high point of this experience comes in 1224: this is the famous event of the vision of the 'man like a seraph' on a cross, and the appearance of the stigmata, later immortalised by Giotto in the frescoes of the Basilica built over Francis' tomb.[4] According to the *Life* by Thomas of Celano, Francis was staying at the hermitage on the mountain of La Verna. While he was there he saw above him 'in a vision of God' a man 'like a seraph' with six wings, hands outstretched and feet joined, fixed to a cross.[5] In this account, Francis does not understand the vision's meaning, but is filled with a mixture of delight and sadness. He was delighted because of the 'beauty' and 'kind expression' the figure showed him; he was saddened by the suffering of the crucifixion. Francis, confused, continues to ponder the vision 'without any clear understanding', and later, there begin to appear in his hands and feet 'marks of nails', like the ones he had seen on the crucified man-seraph in the vision. Thomas then describes in greater detail these marks: like 'heads of nails' on the inner part of his hands and the upper part of the feet, with 'small pieces of flesh' like the bent ends of nails on the opposite side. His right side 'as if pierced by a lance' was covered with a scar, and leaked blood on his clothing.

Francis himself does not mention this experience in any of his writings, not even in the *Testament* he composed toward the end of his life. Thomas of Celano, in his second *Life* of Francis, speaks of a 'thick veil' with which he covered the marks, and his care in hiding them from observers, even his own brothers, though at least two are mentioned as having seen them during his life.[6] In the account of his death and funeral, the stigmata play an important part as his body is shown to Clare and her sisters at San Damiano, and is then venerated by the people of Assisi. The marks are hailed as 'a new miracle', something they had never 'heard of or read in the Scriptures'.[7]

We cannot say what these marks on his body meant to Francis, since he does not tell us. And even with his great enthusiasm for the 'new miracle' of the stigmata, Thomas of Celano, who seems to report the funeral ceremony as an eyewitness, leaves us with the impression that Francis himself did not understand the vision or its consequences. What impressed observers later was that Francis had died as one 'conformed to Christ'. His compassion for the suffering Christ, like his compassion for the sick at the hospital of San Lazzaro, his tender compassion for creatures, made him seem 'like a man of another age'.[8] From being the lesser brother among his companions, he now became the 'saint'. And Saint Francis would, from this point, play an important role as the model, the exemplar of 'Franciscan spirituality'.

And here we begin to pass from the spirituality of Francis to Franciscan spirituality, because the stigmata became immensely important to Francis' followers immediately after his death.

BONAVENTURE

What we may call a 'mysticism of the cross' serves as an organising principle for Bonaventure's *Major Life* of Francis. He speaks of the 'seven visions of the cross of Christ' that marked the different stages of Francis' life.[9] Following the structure that is also found in *The Soul's Journey*, Bonaventure sees the first six of these as preliminary steps, leading to the summit of La Verna. The greatest of these is the vision of the Seraph and the impression of the marks of the stigmata.

> When the true love of Christ
> *had transformed* his lover *into his image* [2 Corinthians 3:18]
> and the forty days were over
> that he had planned to spend in solitude,
> and the feast of St. Michael the Archangel
> had also arrived,
> the angelic man Francis

came *down from the mountain*, [Matthew 8:1]
bearing with him
the image of the Crucified,
which was depicted not on *tablets of stone* [Exodus 31:18]
or on panels of wood
by the hands of a craftsman,
but engraved in the members of his body
by the finger of the living God. [Exodus 31:18; John 11:27]
Because *it is good to keep hidden*
the secret of the King, [Tobit 12:7]
Francis,
aware that he had been given a royal secret,
to the best of his powers
kept the sacred stigmata hidden.
Since it is for God to reveal for his own glory
the wonders which he has performed,
the Lord himself,
who had secretly imprinted those marks on Francis,
publicly worked through them
a number of miracles
so that the miraculous though hidden
power of the stigmata
might be made manifest
by the brightness of divine signs.[10]

Rather than Francis who points toward the cross of Christ, here the tradition points toward Francis himself as the one bearing the marks, signs or image of Christ. This is part of a wider phenomenon in the Franciscan tradition, that of Francis as the way toward the Way who is Christ. In fact, Bonaventure uses his understanding of the stigmata event as the organising principle of *The Soul's Journey into God.*

ANGELA OF FOLIGNO

Angela, Bonaventure's contemporary, testifies to both of these currents in the Franciscan tradition: devotion to Francis and

devotion to the crucified Christ. The description of her earliest
ecstatic experience may help us to understand how Francis
and Christ were related in her perception. She had gone with
a group of companions on a pilgrimage from Foligno to the
great Basilica of St Francis in Assisi, his final burial place.
After an initial visit to the church, she returned, as she
recounts:

> Then, on this second time, as soon as I had genuflected at
> the entrance of the church and when I saw a stained-glass
> window depicting St Francis being closely held by Christ,
> I heard him telling me: 'Thus I will hold you closely to me
> and much more closely than can be observed with the eyes
> of the body.'[11]

Paul Lachance, in his study of Angela's mysticism, says,
'Angela's passionate love affair with "the suffering God-man,"
the crucified Christ, is the central and organising principle
of her journey.'[12] In her *Memorial* she uses the language of
tenderness and affection to describe this love affair. Her mysticism, like that of other Franciscan mystics, speaks from the
heart, and seems to echo that mixture of joy and compassion
that others noticed in Francis.

Angela describes another experience of union with the crucified, which seems a fulfilment of that promise she earlier
received in the Basilica of St Francis in Assisi.

> Once I was at Vespers and was gazing at the cross. And
> while I was thus gazing at the cross with the eyes of the
> body, suddenly my soul was set ablaze with love; and every
> member of my body felt it with the greatest joy. I saw and
> felt that Christ was within me, embracing my soul with
> the very arm with which he was crucified ... At times it
> seems to my soul that it enters into Christ's side, and this
> is a source of great joy and delight; it is indeed such a
> joyful experience to move into Christ's side that in no way
> can I express it and put words to it.[13]

Her joy and delight in the cross, and the importance of the

wound in Christ's side, rendered in a language of tender love, can be found in other authors of the Franciscan tradition, in their meditations on the passion.

JAMES OF MILAN

Brother James was a teacher of theology in Milan, probably in the second half of the thirteenth century. We know little more than this about his life, and for many years even his works were attributed to others, notably to Bonaventure. His great contribution to Franciscan spirituality was the *Stimulus amoris*, a series of meditations on the passion of Christ. (It was translated into English in the fourteenth century by the English mystic, Walter Hilton.) The *Stimulus* deals with the life of perfection with contemplation at its summit. The title itself recalls the stick used by a farmer to 'goad' a team of oxen. The only goad really capable of making a person follow the way of the Lord is love.

But the figure of Francis is not the basis for this meditation, as he is invoked only in an opening prayer. And the theology is not the Christocentric and trinitarian theology of Francis, but is rather typically Scholastic. But the affective and tender approach to the sufferings of Christ, dominated by a deep sense of love and peace, is in perfect harmony with other texts of the Franciscan tradition.[14]

One image that occurs also in other Franciscan mystics, notably Angela, is that of 'entering the wound' in Christ's side, in an experience of mystical union.

> O most beloved wounds of my Lord Jesus Christ! Once on entering them with my eyes open, they were filled with blood. Seeing nothing else, I began to enter, feeling my way into the depths of the inner organs of his charity which surrounded me on every side and deprived me of any possibility of turning back. Here I live, nourishing myself with food that nourishes Him, becoming inebriated with his drink. I am immersed in a sweetness so great

that I am unable to tell you. He who out of love for sinners stayed in the womb of the Virgin now deigns to carry poor me within his inner parts. But I am greatly afraid that the moment of birth will come, depriving me of the delights which I now enjoy. In any case, if he delivers me, he must suckle me at his breast like a mother, wash me with his hands, carry me in his arms, console me with kisses and caress me in his lap. But I know what I shall do: Let him deliver me! His wounds are always open, and through them I will once again enter his womb. And I will keep doing this without tiring until I shall be inseparably one with him.[15]

Wound and womb, delivery and birth, suckling and caressing: these images evoke 'Jesus as Mother', a popular theme of Cistercian authors, among others, in the twelfth and thirteenth centuries.[16] Here they accompany a dramatically physical description of contemplative 'unseeing', in a darkness which is that of life-giving blood.

BARTHOLOMEW OF PISA

Between 1385 and 1390 Bartholomew of Pisa (d. *c*.1401) wrote a book that became immensely popular for its portrayal of the life of Francis and the life of Christ. It represents the apogee of that tendency already noted earlier, of seeing Francis, especially the Francis of the stigmata, as 'another Christ'. The book was entitled, 'The Conformity of the Life of Blessed Francis to the Life of the Lord Jesus'.[17] From his birth to his death, events in the life of Francis are shown as 'conformities' to the gospel accounts of the life of Jesus, to other figures of the Old and New Testaments, in sometimes exhausting detail (the Latin edition runs to over one thousand pages). A good example of the style of these parallels is the following:

Admirable and great was God's creating heaven and earth; but even greater having created a man of such holiness . . . Great the creating of Adam to His image and likeness;

but even greater having transformed Francis in His
perfect, bodily image ... Great and admirable was the
apparition of God to Moses on Mount Sinai and the giving
of the Law; greater was the vision of Christ that Francis
had on the mountain of La Verna and the confirmation of
the evangelical Rule with the seal of the stigmata ... It
was admirable that Christ was crucified by others with
nails of iron; but even greater that Francis was marked
with the stigmata by the same Christ and crucified with
nails of flesh.[18]

Such statements may seem exaggerated to the modern reader,
but did not scandalise readers in the fifteenth century. The
text was widely distributed and appreciated. But with the
beginning of the Reformation, this type of language evoked a
strong reaction. The 'conformities' were satirised by Erasmus
Alber, a disciple of Martin Luther, in the first edition of the
Alcoranus Franciscanorum ('The Koran of the Franciscans') in
1542. In the same year, the first German edition was published
in Wittenberg, with Martin Luther's preface, with the title:
Der Barfüsser Mönche Eulenspiegel und Alcoran ('The Buffoon
and the Koran of the Barefoot Monks'). The *Alcoran* issued a
stinging critique of popular Catholic veneration of saints, sin-
gling out the cult of Francis as *alter Christus*, 'another Christ',
as a prime example of an exaggeration mixed with crude super-
stition.

CAMILLA BATTISTA VARANO

Camilla Battista Varano (d. 1524) became a Poor Clare at
Urbino in 1481, at the age of twenty-three, despite opposition
from her father and problems of health. She returned to
Camerino in 1484 as abbess of a new monastery there. Among
her works are 'Memories of Christ' (*Ricordi di Cristo*), written
at Urbino in 1483, and the 'Mental Sufferings of Christ' (*I
dolori mentali di Cristo*), composed at Camerino in 1488, and

in 1491 an autobiography entitled 'The Spiritual Life' (*Vita spirituale*).[19]

From her autobiography we have the following passage, revealing both the continuing affective character of Franciscan spirituality, as well as the continuing concentration on the suffering Christ. She is visited by the Seraphim, and her heart burns with the desire to 'leave the prison of the body to be with Christ'.

> Violently troubled in soul and body by this burning desire, I wept and moaned bitterly, begging God to free me from the misery of the body and the world. Then while I was praying one day it seemed to me that the blessed Christ was showing me great compassion, and with his arm was hugging my soul to his most holy breast, saying repeatedly, 'Don't cry so much.' And with his other hand he dried the tears of my soul, because this crying was of the soul, not of the body, though I still cried abundant bodily tears. The sweet words of Christ did not stop my weeping, in fact my whole self melted into tears, and I begged him all the more to free me from this bodily prison. Finally he said, 'I can't, not yet.' And he showed me his most powerful hands, tied in many places, and said: 'These are the prayers of the sisters and brothers who offer them so that you do not die. Be patient.'[20]

Here we reach a classic motif of the spirituality of 'denial of the world', that already seems far from the love of the other 'brothers and sisters' in the world of creation that forms such an important part of the popular picture of Francis. In fact, as the Catholic Reformation and the Inquisition make their presence felt, especially after the Council of Trent, many of the features once characteristic of Franciscan spirituality were adopted by other spiritual writers of the time. Another way to view this development is to say that by the sixteenth century themes from the Franciscan tradition (especially an emphasis on the passion of Christ) had become commonplace in Catholic spirituality, and were no longer identifiably 'Franciscan'.

7. 'BE PRAISED, MY LORD, WITH ALL YOUR CREATURES'

One of the most common representations of Francis today is 'the saint in the birdbath'. Usually with a bird perched on his shoulder, sometimes with squirrels and rabbits at his feet, the *Poverello* has become a figure of garden *kitsch*. Despite the superficiality and sentimentality of these figures, they do represent the continuation of a long artistic tradition that began shortly after his death. Francis struck the popular religious imagination of his day as unusual for the prominence of nature, especially animals, in the stories told about him.[1]

As in regard to poverty, so also in regard to creatures we must remember the motivation for Francis' words and actions. He was not simply a lover of Nature, though since the nineteenth century he has often been seen as that. Reflecting on his own words in the 'Canticle of Creatures' we can begin to see how these fellow creatures, his brothers and sisters, reflected to him the face of the beloved Son.

Francis knows himself through the incarnate Son: he also sees the rest of creation in this same light. All creatures, not just human beings, come from this same source, the good God of the Trinity, and all come through the same medium, the Son. The one through whom all things were created has come to be one of the creatures. Here is the foundation for the remarkable interest, respect and affection Francis shows toward all creatures. They are, with Francis, 'fellow creatures' with the incarnate Son of God, and are therefore 'brothers and sisters' to Francis.

CREATION AND CONTEMPLATION

His own 'Canticle of the Creatures', a poem set to music and sung with his brothers, gives us a glimpse of his relationship with other creatures. 'Be praised, my Lord, with all your creatures, especially Sir Brother Sun ... he bears a likeness of You, Most High.' Sister Moon and stars, Brothers Fire and Wind, Sister Water and 'our Sister Mother Earth' follow one another in the litany of praise, resembling the 'Canticle of the Three Young Men' in the Book of Daniel (3:57–88).

The Canticle, in the medieval dialect of Umbria, is addressed to 'You, my Lord', with the recurring phrase *'lodato si per'*, which in English can be rendered 'be praised by' or 'be praised for' each of the creatures. As these brothers and sisters are named, a brief description is given for each. Brother Sun 'illumines us'; Sister Moon and Stars are 'beautiful, clear and precious', like jewels; Brother Fire 'lights up the night'; Sister Mother Earth produces 'fruits and coloured flowers and herbs'.

After moving through the cosmic elements of earth, air, fire and water, Francis gives praise for his human brothers and sisters: those who pardon; those who endure suffering; those who keep peace. Francis added the final verses, we learn from Thomas of Celano, as he prepared to die: 'Be praised, My Lord, for our Sister bodily Death', with woe for those who die in sin, and blessing for those who die in 'Your most holy will'.

In this Canticle we hear in Francis' own words his tenderness toward the world around him, a world he observed carefully. When placed against the backdrop of world-denying or dualist religious movements of the time, such as Catharism, this celebration of the world as place of brother–sister relationships stands out in even bolder relief.

'He discerned the hidden things of nature with his sensitive heart,' as Thomas of Celano expresses it.[2] People around Francis had noticed his reverence and tender affection for all creatures, calling each of them 'brother' or 'sister'. Knowing Francis' Canticle makes it easier for us to understand the numerous stories told in early documents about his love for creatures. Some of his early companions gave stories to Brother Thomas for use in writing his *Life*. They mention Francis' reverence, affection and joy in the presence of many different creatures:

> Francis abounded in the spirit of charity; he was filled with compassion not only toward men in need, but even toward dumb animals, reptiles, birds, and other creatures, sensible and insensible.
>
> . . . How great a gladness do you think the beauty of the flowers brought to his mind when he saw the shape of their beauty and perceived the odor of their sweetness? . . . When he found an abundance of flowers, he preached to them and invited them to praise the Lord as though they were endowed with reason. In the same way he exhorted with the sincerest purity cornfields and vineyards, stones and forests and all the beautiful things of the fields, fountains of water and the green things of the gardens, earth and fire, air and wind, to love God and serve him willingly.[3]

In three related incidents, Thomas shows Francis being given a rabbit, a fish and 'a waterfowl'. In each case, Francis holds the animal 'affectionately', and calls it by name: 'brother'. He 'rejoices' and then is caught up in prayer (an odd contemplative moment: sitting in a boat on a lake, holding a duck, happily swept away in God). 'Returning to himself' (as if he had been in a kind of ecstasy) he allows the animal to go free. Just touching or holding an animal, a fish or a bird, can send Francis into a kind of rapture because they were created through Christ and for him. They bear traces of him. They are reminders, messages, messengers from Francis' lover.

THE FIORETTI

Among those texts that derive from oral traditions circulating among Francis' followers is the classic of Italian literature, *I Fioretti di san Francesco*, 'The Little Flowers of Saint Francis'.[4] This is a late fourteenth-century translation of the Latin *Actus*

beati Francisci et sociorum eius ('The Deeds of Blessed Francis
and His Companions'), probably written by Ugolino da Monte-
giorgio between 1327 and 1340. More than any other text, the
Fioretti has shaped the popular image of Francis the lover of
animals, the mystic of nature.

To give examples of the freshness and vigour of these
legends, we may choose two, the first about very meek creatures and the second about a very fierce one.

A young man had caught many wild doves and was going to
sell them in the market. Saint Francis met him on the road.
'He always had special pity on meek animals', so with a 'merciful eye on those doves' he said to the young man:

> O good young man, please give them to me, for such inno-
> cent birds are compared in the Scripture to chaste, humble
> and faithful souls, and should not fall into the hands of
> cruel people who will kill them.

The young man gives Francis the doves, and he, 'holding
them to his heart' and 'speaking sweetly to them', says:

> O my sisters, simple doves, innocent and chaste, why do
> you let yourselves get caught? See, now I want to save you
> from death and make nests for you, so that you may bear
> fruit and multiply according to the commandments of our
> Creator.

He prepared nests for them, and as they became used to their
new quarters 'they started to lay eggs and raise their children
there among the friars'. 'They grew so tame with Saint Francis
and the other friars that they seemed like chickens the friars
had raised.'[5]

The charming simplicity of the story helps to account for the
popularity these tales enjoyed, as they passed from teller to
listener during the century after Francis' death. The best
known of all the legends in the *Fioretti* is undoubtedly the
next one, about a wild and threatening beast.

'A very fierce wolf' had terrorised the people of Gubbio, and
Francis came to their aid. As Francis went out to meet it, the

wolf 'with his mouth wide open' came toward the saint. Francis made the sign of the cross, and called the wolf to himself: 'Brother Wolf, come here. I command you on behalf of Christ that you do no harm to me nor to anyone.' The 'terrible wolf' closed its jaws and did not run away. 'It became as meek as a lamb, and lay down at the feet of Saint Francis.'

Francis then had the wolf and the townspeople make peace (Brother Wolf indicating his consent by wagging his tail and nodding his head). The wolf agreed to do no further harm and, since it was hunger that made him so ferocious (as Francis explained to the disconcerted citizens), the people of Gubbio would have to agree to feed him for the rest of his life. To seal the 'peace treaty', at Francis' request 'the wolf lifted up his right paw and placed it in the hand of Saint Francis'. And so the story of the 'very fierce wolf of Gubbio' ends, 'to the glory of Jesus Christ and of the Little Poor Man Francis, Amen'.[6]

The *Fioretti* show us the popular image of the saint who loved animals, communicated with them and tamed them, evoking the classic theme of Christian hagiography of the saint who returns to the state of Paradise.[7] But the Franciscan tradition also worked with those insights about Francis and his love for creation in theological language, at the theological centre of the Middle Ages, the University of Paris.

CREATION IN BONAVENTURE

Francis' deep appreciation of Christ as the centre of creation found its theological spokesman in Bonaventure.[8] Zachary Hayes has explained that Christ became increasingly the central concern of Bonaventure's theology over the years. 'The core of the Christological mystery is the fact that in Jesus the center of all reality has become incarnate and has been made historically visible.'[9]

Meditating on the ways in which we might be able to understand this work of Christ-centred creation, Bonaventure uses the language of the 'exemplar', as we might use the term 'prototype' or 'model'. God is the exemplar of all things; the humanity of Jesus is the expression of the exemplar; all creation is formed in Christ. Bonaventure uses the homely example of a thirteenth-century (probably Parisian) artisan to clarify his thought:

> One [exemplar] is interior, in the mind of the artist, as the cause according to which the artist produces his works. The other is exterior; it is that to which one who is ignorant of art looks and by which he is directed in a certain way, just as mechanical artists have certain forms external to themselves according to which they direct their works, as is clear in the case of shoemakers.[10]

Christ is the prototype, model or exemplar: the well-made shoe on the shoemaker's worktable, or on God's universal worktable of creation. Every part of creation and every creature has as its model Jesus, the Christ, the Word incarnate. In this way Bonaventure makes sense of the creation, following the example of Francis, as a way toward God, through Christ, and not as an obstacle to be overcome in the search for God. He incorporates reflection on the world of creatures into his overall plan of Franciscan mystical theology, in the *Soul's Journey*, likening the creation to one of the steps in the ascent toward the summit of contemplation.

From the first two stages [of the journey]
in which we are led to behold God
in vestiges,
like the two wings covering the Seraph's feet, [cf. Isaiah 6:2]
we can gather that all the creatures of the sense world
lead the mind
of the contemplative and wise man
to the eternal God.
For these creatures are
shadows, echoes and pictures
of that first, most powerful, most wise and most perfect
principle,
of that eternal Source, light and Fullness,

of that efficient, exemplary and ordering Art.
They are
vestiges, representations, spectacles
proposed to us
and signs divinely given
so that we can see God.[11]

Bonaventure developed a theological tradition in which creation can become the means toward the discovery of Christ. The task of continuing it would be left to one of his successors, John Duns Scotus, and to modern interpreters of Franciscan 'creation theology'. But before we consider that theological side of the question, we should also attend to other witnesses who testify to a living, though still inchoate, grasp of Francis' intuition that the world (creation, creatures, nature) holds within itself a revelation of the Creator, waiting to be brought to light.

ANGELA'S MYSTICAL VISION OF CREATION

Though not a theologian in academic terms, Angela was considered a 'teacher of theologians' (for example, Ubertino da Casale) because of her vivid expressions of the experience of God. Though her ecstatic visions often concerned the sufferings of Christ, the created world around her also had its special place in her mystical experience. In the following passage she describes an 'indescribable experience' of the world filled with God, an echo of the 'Canticle of the Creatures'.

Afterward [God] added: 'I want to show you something of my power.' And immediately the eyes of my soul were opened, and in a vision I beheld the fullness of God in which I beheld and comprehended the whole of creation, that is, what is on this side and what is beyond the sea, the abyss, the sea itself, and everything else. And in everything that I saw, I could perceive nothing except the presence of the power of God, and in a manner totally indescribable. And my soul in an excess of wonder cried

out: 'This world is pregnant with God!' Wherefore I understood how small is the whole of creation – that is, what is
on this side and what is beyond the sea, the abyss, the
sea itself, and everything else – but the power of God fills
it all to overflowing.[12]

This sense of a world so filled with God that it seems about to
give birth may have its corollary in the later theories of Scotus
about the incarnation; in this sense, the world is longing to
give birth to the Creator, it is constantly in the process of
giving birth to the incarnate Word, its Image. Or, in Bonaventure's words, 'Every creature is a word of God because it speaks
of God.'[13]

CREATION IN SCOTUS

Heir to Bonaventure's role as a leader of Franciscan theologians, Scotus understands creation as deriving from the
goodness of God and the grandeur of the incarnation. He
reflects the view already so simply expressed by Francis' rep-
etitions of God as 'good, good, good'. In a prayer at the opening
of his work on 'God as First Principle', Scotus prays, 'You are
infinitely good, communicating the rays of your goodness most
liberally; to you, the most lovable, all things tend, each in its
own way, as to their ultimate end.'[14] Thus all things (human
beings, all of creation) are 'naturally inclined' toward loving
totally that infinite good, which is God.[15] And this good God
toward whom all things tend is love, not just in outward
expression of charity toward creatures, but also intrinsically:
the self-identity of God (to use a modern term) is love or
charity.[16] In considering the views of Manichaeans (probably
the Cathars of southern France), Scotus posed a question that
reveals something of his Franciscan intuition: 'Can't they see
that every being, just as a being, is good?'[17]

The great contribution of Scotus was that of offering a theor-
etical framework for a spirituality of creation that would be
developed later. In the Franciscan tradition after Scotus, the

theme of creation as a component of spirituality declines in importance. Preachers take *exempla*, morally instructive stories, from the natural world but not because of any apparent interest in the creatures described: their point, like that of the fables of Aesop or Montaigne, is to instruct their listeners concerning vices and virtues, and the phenomena of nature, especially animal behaviour, serve that purpose well.

We have already mentioned that Francis was considered 'new' by his contemporaries. His 'new' attitude toward the created world would have to wait several centuries after Scotus to be discovered anew, among writers who were, for the most part, not Franciscans themselves.

RECOVERY OF THE FRANCISCAN SPIRITUALITY OF CREATION

In the nineteenth century a new interest in Francis and a new interest in the works of Scotus combined to revive the theme of nature, first outside, then inside the Franciscan movement. Early in the nineteenth century Joseph Görres, the German Romantic, published his work on Francis, the lyrical troubadour, admirer of Nature and poet of creation.[18] In 1852, in France, Fréderic Ozanam, founder of the St Vincent de Paul Society, wrote on the poetry of Franciscan authors, with selections from the *Fioretti*, the 'Little Flowers of St Francis'.[19] These works began to point to Francis as a saint whose love for Nature made him a kind of Catholic icon for values espoused by Romantic poets and philosophers. It would be the great contribution of an English poet, and a Welsh library, to bring the emerging interest in natural observation and scientific investigation into dialogue with the writings of Scotus, and thus back into the consciousness of the Franciscan tradition.

THE OXFORD CONNECTION

On 3 August 1872, a group of Jesuit scholastics arrived on the Isle of Man for a holiday. One of them noted in his journal:

> At this time I had first begun to get hold of the copy of Scotus on the Sentences in the Baddely library and was flush with a new stroke of enthusiasm. It may come to nothing or it may be a mercy from God.

His journal entry for that day continues, 'But just then when I took in any inscape of the sky or sea I thought of Scotus.'[20]

That Jesuit writing on his holiday on the Isle of Man was Gerard Manley Hopkins (d. 1889). A convert to Rome from the Church of England, Hopkins entered the Jesuit novitiate shortly after completing a brilliant undergraduate career at Oxford. With his training in late nineteenth-century Catholic theology, the Scholasticism of the manuals, and within the strongly anti-worldly spirituality of his time, Hopkins felt himself morally or spiritually misformed because of his fascination and delight with specific, individual things, especially the things of nature, a fascination observed by others. A Jesuit brother who had lived at Stonyhurst while Hopkins was a student there, remembers him in this way:

> One of Hopkins's special delights was the path from the Seminary to the College. After a shower, he would run and crouch down to gaze at the crushed quartz glittering as the sun came out again. 'Ay, a strange young man, crouching down that gate to stare at some wet sand. A fair natural 'e seemed to us, that Mr 'opkins.'[21]

This fascination, this sensual delight in the things of nature, became a problem for Hopkins, something he felt must be suppressed or disciplined through asceticism, in order to conform himself to the search for 'heavenly things', 'the things that are above'. It was a 'mercy of God' that during his theology days he came across the works of Scotus in the library of the Jesuit theologate at St Beuno's in Wales. Like Scotus, Hopkins had been a brilliant Oxford scholar. This 'Oxford connection' would later inspire one of Hopkins' poems, 'Duns Scotus' Oxford'. J. Hillis Miller, in a fine study of Hopkins and Christology, wrote:

> Ultimately, with the help of Scotus and other theologians, Hopkins broadens his theory of the Incarnation until he comes to see all things as created in Christ.[22]

This was a revelation. It was also the solution to that severe problem of conscience that had plagued Hopkins since his becoming a Roman Catholic. On reading Scotus he found a theologically positive view of the specific and individual. He discovered Christ in matter. This discovery he expressed both in his poetry and in the prose of his journals. One of those journal entries speaks of this new-found, relaxed delight in nature: 'As we drove home the stars came out thick: I leant back to look at them and my heart opening more than usual praised our Lord to and in whom all that beauty comes home.'[23]

Hopkins' poetry itself may be seen as an example of Scotus' understanding of the incarnation. The poet attends to the specific, even the minutest details, like the tiny, crushed quartz crystals of the sand in the path at Stonyhurst. The reason that makes sense, in view of the Franciscan tradition, is because the tiny grains of sand are eucharistic, with a small 'e', if you like, but truly eucharistic, the extension of the incarnation in matter.

Listen to some selections from Hopkins' journals where he records his observations of natural phenomena:

> below the sun it was like clear oil but just as full of colour, shaken over with slanted flashing 'travellers,' all in flight, stepping one behind the other, their edges tossed with bright ravelling, as if white napkins were thrown up in the sun but not quite at the same moment so that they were all in a scale down the air falling one after the other to the ground.[24]

The key to resolving 'the problem of Nature' that the Jesuit

Hopkins found in the Franciscan Scotus was fundamentally the person of the incarnate Word. The humanity of Jesus, even more emphatically the body of Jesus, is the point of God's creating everything, the exemplary cause of creation, to use Bonaventure's language. This is the model on which God models everything else: those white napkins of sunlight, stars, snails, raindrops, oxygen, magnesium, protons, grapes, volcanoes: each of them and the relation each has with every other thing is rooted in that cause. They do something. What they do is, in odd language, themselves: they do them-selves. The grape grapes, the star stars, a volcano volcanoes. Each, doing this, is being itself: doing what it is. Hopkins calls this 'do-being'.

This do-being is doing-Christ. That is what they were formed to do. This can be difficult to understand: perhaps it is also difficult to experience. It may be best to say what this is *not* before trying to say what it is. And then we can talk a bit more about the 'why' of this.

What is *not* the relation between the grain of sand and Christ? The sand-grain is not just a symbol of Christ, though it can be that if we work at it. But that requires that it 'stand for' something about Christ. We may decide that the grain of sand, because it is small, makes us think of the humility of Christ. This is a very familiar use of religious language, but by thinking in this way what have we done? We have abstracted, identified an adjective about the sand-grain ('small') with an adjective about Christ ('humble'). We have taken a quality of a thing and associated it with some quality of Christ. But the sand-grain itself is not all that important: a small acorn or a small tomato could do the job just as well. They are dispensable, interchangeable. They are *used* to achieve some other purpose, to teach a lesson, usually a moral lesson. And here we would be once again on the familiar territory of the preacher's moral *exempla*.

And whether we use the sand, the acorn or the tomato, the *thing* can produce only reference to some quality or aspect of Christ, 'humility', or some other description *about* Christ. This is perfectly fine to do, of course, but it can get tiresome. It is theologically based on the more common Thomistic view of nature founded on the theory of analogy of being. True being exists only in God, and all other being is derivative, pointing toward true being, but only weakly and indirectly.

What fires Hopkins (though he only comes to articulate it through reading Scotus) is that the sand-grain, by being/doing itself, directly, immediately *does* the creating Word incarnate: Christ. And it does that quite well without my sitting and cogitating about 'small' or 'humble'. Here is Hopkins painting this perception in poem number 34:

> As kingfishers catch fire, dragonflies draw flame;
>> As tumbled over rim in roundy wells
>> Stones ring; like each tucked string tells, each hung bell's
> Bow swung finds tongue to fling out broad its name;
> Each mortal thing does one Thing and the same:
>> Deals out that being indoors each one dwells;
>> Selves – goes itself; *myself* it speaks and spells,
> Crying *What I do is me: for that I came.*[25]

What is Christ-full is the sand doing sand: it is noun become verb and not adjective. And the sand-grain sanding is doing *all* the beauty that is Christ, not just this or that aspect of him, smallness or humility or whatever.

This expresses the profound notion of Scotus known as the 'univocity of being'. This subject has been explored by several scholars, including Fr Allan Wolter.[26] We might say that this perception, common to both Scotus and Hopkins, allows for a direct connection between our awareness of a thing and our awareness of Christ. J. Hillis Miller explains this more precisely:

> The idea of the univocity of being leads to a different view of nature (from that of Thomism), and therefore to a different kind of poetry. In this view natural things, instead of having a derived being, participate directly in

the being of the creator. They are in the same way that
he is. Each created thing, in its own special way, is the
total image of its creator. It expresses not some aspect of
God, but his beauty as a whole. Such a view of nature
leads to a poetry in which things are not specific symbols,
but all mean one thing and the same: the beauty of Christ,
in whom they are created.[27]

In his journals Hopkins makes the following entry that renders
this idea rather well: 'I do not think I have ever seen anything
more beautiful than the bluebell I have been looking at. I know
the beauty of our Lord by it.'[28]

It seems to me that this requires a different kind of discipline
of the observer/participant of Nature, whether you or me or
Hopkins. The task is not to get lots of ideas about creatures
that can then be lined up with ideas about Christ. The task,
which is essentially contemplative, is to observe closely, attentively, carefully that things are/do themselves. That doing/being
is their doing/being Christ.

Again, in Hopkins' own words:

> the just man justices;
> Kéeps gráce: that keeps all his goings graces;
> Acts in God's eye what in God's eye he is –
> Christ – [29]

It is each thing, individual, particular, which does this being-
Christ. This grape be/does Christ in dark purple on the left-
hand side as I face it, while more crimson mixed with mauve
on the right side, where it has a fine dusting of grey-brown
near the stem where the mould is. Put simply, it is/does only
its own grape, not the one next to it or above it in the bunch.
We notice its uniqueness when we look at it carefully.

In her work on Hopkins, *The Dragon in the Gate*,[30] Elisabeth
W. Schneider gives an example of this minute observation from
Hopkins' journal:

> Oaks: the organisation of this tree is difficult. Speaking
> generally no doubt the determining planes are concentric,

a system of brief contiguous and continuous tangents, whereas those of the cedar would roughly be called horizontals and those of the beech radiating but modified by droop and by a screw-set towards jutting points. But beyond this since the normal growth of the boughs is radiating and the leaves grow some way in there is of course a system of spoke-wise clubs of green – sleeve-pieces . . . Oaks differ much, and much turns on the broadness of the leaf, the narrower giving the crisped and starry and Catherine-wheel forms, the broader the flat-pieced mailed or shard-covered ones in which it is possible to see composition in dips etc on wider bases than the single knot or cluster. But I shall study them further.

Schneider tells us that he did exactly that, and in a journal entry eight days later declared, 'I have now found the law of the oak leaves.'[31]

Here we touch the Scotistic notion of *haecceitas*, being this thing and not that next thing that resembles it rather closely. In the more common Thomistic view that Hopkins studied, things have two fundamental components, matter and form. The form in this case is 'grapeness' and the matter is the physical attributes of sweetness, roundness, sugars and skin. Scotus adds a third component: being *this* grape: *haec*, 'this'. Here is the corollary of the incarnation: the eternal Word became incarnate as *this* Jewish carpenter's son: the unique, unrepeatable, specific creature is the incarnate Creator.

In this Scotistic view, close, even minute, observation and attention to *things* is revelatory. This is a truly contemplative act. A deep gazing *into* things can allow glimpses of Christ. The close analogy is that of traditional eucharistic devotion, gazing on the consecrated bread of the Eucharist, pondering the invitation, '*Ecce Agnus Dei*', 'Behold (that is, *look* and *see*) Christ': baked wheat flour, juice of grapes crushed. Here is ordinary Near Eastern food: see the Creator of the universe.

In a similar way, gaze on this leaf, this stone, this molecule, this hand, this shadowy light streaming through this window, and *Ecce*, Behold! (Hopkins would say *inscape!*) Look and *see*: creature and Creator marvellously *one-d*, co-present, with no loss of identity for the creature or the Creator.

As Hopkins wrote to a friend, 'I think that the trivialness of life is, and personally to each one, ought to be seen to be, done away with by the Incarnation.'[32]

8. THE FRANCISCAN TRADITION TODAY

This book is destined to be among the last of many works on Franciscan spirituality published in the twentieth century and, hopefully, among the first to be read in the twenty-first. Like a previous study of the Franciscan movement, this one is being completed in the Piedmont region of northern Italy.[1] Here, in the *Valli Valdesi*, the movement founded by Peter Waldo, a contemporary of Francis and Clare, lives on in the Waldensian churches. Franciscans, men and women, secular and religious, live here too, following a 'form of life' initiated in Assisi, far to the south, eight centuries ago. In this place and at this time I would like to offer a summary of the Franciscan tradition that, like the ancient Roman deity Janus, ancient patron of nearby Genoa, looks from the present backward, at what has been, while looking forward, toward what is to come.

Should the Franciscan tradition teach people to recreate the experience of a Francis or a Clare? Certainly not. The attempt would be fruitless and frustrating. And even if it could succeed, then, like Francis and Clare themselves, it would have to be dead. It continues to be a living tradition today because others have carried on the tradition, in new times and places, in their own words and example. Francis presents us with one example, a moving and inspiring example, but the tradition does not stop with him. In his words, 'I have done what was mine to do, may Christ now show you what is yours.' Francis wished that his whole life would point to Christ. To stop at Francis would be to frustrate the intention he had for his followers. Clare also pointed away from herself, holding up the Mirror who is Christ, and indicating Francis as the one who showed her that Mirror. But both Clare and Francis, in their words and gestures, reveal to us, sometimes clearly, sometimes obscurely, intuitions about God-become-human that still remain profoundly challenging. That is the only reason for writing a book like this in our day: to express those intuitions in a language understandable to today's sincere Christian believer and religious seeker.

What can the medieval Francis and Clare mean today? And what is there in the long Franciscan tradition that merits attention today?

We usually ask questions of the past because we are searching for answers in the present. In the field of spirituality today there is an explosion of interest in the sacred, in ritual, in the recovery of the body and the sacredness of the earth, in the language of women's voices, and in the rediscovery of community. Sometimes with too great facility proponents of one or the other tradition lay claim to one or all of these areas as the special terrain of their spirituality. I wish to avoid giving that impression in regard to the Franciscan tradition. Instead, I would like to suggest a possible service that the tradition of Francis and Clare can offer to those who are searching for God, or simply for a sense of meaning in their lives.

The Franciscan tradition can and should begin by doing a 'disservice' to the interest in spirituality today. Forms of spirituality, broadly defined as interest in the spiritual, can sometimes be the search for religious experience that takes us away from ourselves, the daily activities of life, the world, the mundane. Some techniques of concentration or ritual point their practitioners toward a completely pure, other, spiritual reality that is characterised by utter lack of feeling, images or materiality. This world and our lives must then be inevitably inferior, if not unreal, in view of that other realm of 'soul' or bliss, or spiritual being. Such a view alienates rather than integrates spirituality and life as we live it daily.

To this type of spirituality the Franciscan tradition can offer its disservice by pointing to feet. These are the 'dirty feet' of the incarnate Word.[2] Following the example of Francis and

Clare, the Franciscan tradition today can point instead to the 'down-to-earth-ness' of the experience of God, who has made an irrevocable decision to be incarnate.

This is also a service offered to others who are deeply concerned about an interest in spirituality that seduces people away from the pressing needs of contemporary society. A spirituality with consistent emphasis on the God who is revealed in Christ enfleshed, 'in-mattered', and in history, can offer a point of dialogue with those who see in much of the contemporary religious quest a denial of responsibility for the world in which we live.

The world at the end of the 1900s is marked by the stark contrast between the affluence of a few individuals and societies and the misery of the majority of others. In such a world, what value can poverty have, a focal point of the Franciscan tradition? Believing or preaching that poverty itself has some value is as meaningless today as it was in the thirteenth century, and can be used to justify evils perpetrated on the poor. As I hope to have made clear in the preceding pages, poverty itself can never be a value. It is the relinquishment of wealth, status and domination over others that the incarnation teaches Francis and Clare in their pursuit of the 'holy poverty' of Jesus. Following this example, living *sine proprio*, without anything of one's own, today implies the refusal to arrogate to one's self what belongs to all, because all belongs to the Creator. Everything is gift, nothing is 'property'. The gospel mandate to 'sell all and give to the poor', which Francis and Clare followed, far from being meaningless, is as urgent in our own day as it was in theirs.

The recovery of a spirituality of creation, linked with contemporary awareness of the global effects of environmental exploitation, can form a bridge between contemporary concerns and this wisdom from the past. For Christians as well as other people of spirit, the world has become a problem or, better said, the effects of human appropriation of the earth have become the problem. In the gentle and non-possessive respect toward 'brother' and 'sister' water, air, fire and 'our

Sister Mother Earth', Francis, the patron saint of ecology, can help point us toward a community of creation in which humans take seriously the role of being 'lesser', and 'subject to every creature because of God'.

Not least importantly, the spirituality of reconciliation, so evident in Francis' peaceful dialogue with Malek el-Kamil during the Fifth Crusade, reminds us of what has been called 'The Spirit of Assisi', a spirit of respectful and attentive dialogue among members of differing religious traditions. Wars and threats of war among nations, invoking God as their justification, contradict that Franciscan understanding of 'the Most High' God who is 'good, all good, the highest good'. In the figure of the *Poverello* those who continue to struggle for reconciliation among nations and individuals may find a sign of hope. Whenever he spoke to people, or birds, or wolves, he always began with these words, with which I end: 'May the Lord give you peace.'

NOTES

Introduction

1. Martial Lekeux OFM, 'Note on the Caritas Series' in *Franciscan Mysticism*, tr. Dom Basil Whelman OSB (London: Sheed and Ward, 1928; Pulaski, Wisconsin: Franciscan Publishers, repr. 1956), pp. 1–2.
2. Balancing these two dimensions, individual authors or texts and broad themes, presents a challenge to anyone studying or writing in the field of Christian spirituality. A useful model for our task is given by *World Spirituality: An Encyclopedic History of the Religious Quest*, 25 volumes (projected), Ewert Cousins (gen. ed.) (New York: Crossroad, 1985–). By providing thematic essays as well as studies of individual authors and texts, the editors have allowed for both depth and breadth of coverage. The three volumes on Christian spirituality are: Volume 16, *Christian Spirituality: Origins to the Twelfth Century*, ed. Bernard McGinn, John Meyendorff, Jean Leclercq (1985); Volume 17, *Christian Spirituality: High Middle Ages and Reformation*, ed. Jill Raitt (1987); and Volume 18, *Christian Spirituality: Post-Reformation and Modern*, ed. Louis Dupré and Don E. Saliers (1989).
3. A summary of the development of the Franciscan tradition can be found in the article, 'Frères Mineurs' in *Dictionnaire de Spiritualité, Ascetique et Mystique* (Paris: Beauchesne, 1962), vol. V, col. 1268–1422. The first two volumes of an encyclopedic treatment (in Italian) of Franciscan spiritual writers have already appeared. *Scritti dei Mistici Francescani, Secolo XIII (I mistici*, vol. I) (Assisi: Editrici Francescane, 1995); *Mistici Francescani, Secolo XIV* (vol. II) (Assisi: Editrici Francescane, 1997). The series is to include all the significant authors of the Franciscan spiritual tradition, arranged chronologically. Much of the literature on the Franciscan tradition is not (or not yet) available in English but I have indicated English translations in the cases where I know of them.

1. 'To Follow the Footsteps of Our Lord Jesus Christ'

1. The critical edition of early Franciscan documents is: Enrico Menesto', Stefano Brufani et al. (eds.), *Fontes Franciscani* (S. Maria degli

Angeli-Assisi: 1995).

For the writings of Francis and Clare in English, the standard edition in English has been: Regis J. Armstrong, Ignatius Brady (eds.), *Francis and Clare: The Complete Works* (Ramsey NJ: Paulist Press, 1982). For a revised and expanded version of early documents concerning Clare see Regis J. Armstrong (ed.), *Clare of Assisi: Early Documents* (St Bonaventure NY: Franciscan Institute, 1990).

The standard collection of all early sources has been: Marion A. Habig (ed.), *St Francis of Assisi, Writings and Early Biographies: English Omnibus of the Sources for the Life of St Francis* (Chicago: Franciscan Herald Press, 1973).

The new English text of the writings of Francis and early Franciscan texts, based on the new Latin critical edition, is being published contemporaneously with this volume: Regis J. Armstrong, J. A. Wayne Hellmann, William J. Short (eds.), *Francis of Assisi: Early Documents* (3 vols) (New York: New City Press, 1999–).

Early Franciscan sources will be cited using the abbreviations listed at the beginning of this volume. A standard system of numbering is used for these, established by the critical edition in *Fontes Franciscani*. For example, 1Cel 45 refers to the first *Life* of Francis by Thomas of Celano, paragraph 45. Using this standard numbering system for these texts, the reader will find them in all the collections listed above.

2. Test 16.
3. Test 1–3, 5–7, 16–18.
4. RegNb 9:6.
5. The passage is in fact a collage of several versions of the story: Matthew 10:9–10; Luke 9:3, 10:3–4; Mark 6:8.
6. 1Cel 22. The *Anonymous of Perugia* has another, perhaps earlier, version of the story: Francis opens the Gospel book (offered by a priest) three times, finding the three different accounts of the Synoptics, after his first followers arrive (AP 11).
7. RegB 1.
8. RCl 1.
9. A richly documented source for Assisi in the time of Francis and Clare is Arnaldo Fortini, *Francis of Assisi*, tr. Helen Moak (New York: Crossroad, 1981), originally published in five volumes as *Nova Vita di San Francesco* (Santa Maria degli Angeli, Italy: Tipografia Porziuncola, 1959). For a modern biography of Francis based on broad research, see Raoul Manselli, *St Francis of Assisi*, tr. Paul Duggan (Chicago: Franciscan Herald Press, 1988), originally published as *San Francesco d'Assisi* (Rome: Bulzoni, 1980; 2nd rev. edn, 1981). For recent studies of Clare's life and writings, see Ingrid J. Peterson OSF, *Clare of Assisi: A Biographical Study* (Quincy IL: Franciscan Press, 1993); Margaret Carney OSF, *The First Franciscan Woman: Clare of Assisi and Her Form of Life* (Quincy IL: Franciscan Press, 1993);

Marco Bartoli, *Clare of Assisi*, tr. Sister Frances Teresa osc (Quincy IL: Franciscan Press, 1993), originally published as *Chiara d'Assisi* (Rome: Istituto Storico dei Cappuccini, 1989).

10. The First Crusade took Jerusalem out of Islamic control in 1099; the Second ended in defeat at Damascus (1148); the Third (1189–91) and Fourth (1202) occurred during the early lifetime of both Francis and Clare; during the Fifth Crusade (1218–22) Francis met with the leader of the Islamic forces at Damietta, Egypt.

11. Today several of these texts are considered of special importance: *The Anonymous of Perugia*; *The Legend of Perugia / Assisi Compilation*; and *The Legend of the Three Companions*. The complex relationship of Thomas' works to other texts from Francis' early followers has occupied scholars for most of the last century in what is called 'The Franciscan Question'. See Fernando Uribe, 'Cien años de la cuestion Franciscana: Evolución de la problematica', *Antonianum* LXVIII, fasc. 1 (January–March, 1993), pp. 348–74.

12. Proc, Witness 20.

13. LegCl 9.

14. Martial Lekeux ofm, *Short-Cut to Divine Love*, tr. Paul J. Oligny ofm (Chicago: Franciscan Herald Press, 1962), p. 6.

15. See Carolyn Walker Bynum, *Docere verbo et exemplo: An Aspect of Twelfth-Century Spirituality* (Missoula, Mont.: Scholars Press, 1979).

16. 1Cel 97; 2Cel 95.

17. Eric Doyle, 'St Francis of Assisi and the Christocentric Character of Franciscan Life and Doctrine' in Damian McElrath (ed.), *Franciscan Christology* (St Bonaventure NY: Franciscan Institute Publications, 1980), p. 2.

18. L. Moulin, *Vita e governo degli Ordini religiosi* (Milan: Vita e pensiero, 1965), p. 36.

2. 'The Humility of the Incarnation'

1. LaudDei; LaudHor; RegB 23.

2. RegNb 23:1–3.

3. Adm 1:1–4.

4. Adm 5.

5. RegNb 13:1–6.

6. In McElrath, *Franciscan Christology*, p. 7. The reference to Francis' 'Letter to a General Chapter' is the following (EpOrd 13–14): 'the most holy body and blood of our Lord Jesus Christ, in whom all things in heaven and on earth have been made peaceful and reconciled to Almighty God' [cf. Colossians 1:20].

7. 1Cel 84–86.

8. 1Cel 84.

9. 2EpFid 4.

10. 1Cel 84, 85.

11. EpOrd 27–28.
12. SalBVM 1.
13. 2EpFid 4.
14. RegNb 9:5.
15. Sermon II on the Nativity of the Lord, in *What Manner of Man? Sermons on Christ by St Bonaventure*, tr. Zachary Hayes OFM (Chicago: Franciscan Herald Press, 1974), p. 57.
16. *What Manner of Man?* p. 72.
17. *The Soul's Journey into God* in *Bonaventure*, tr. Ewert Cousins (New York: Paulist Press, 1978), p. 111.
18. *The Soul's Journey into God*, p. 62.
19. *The Soul's Journey into God*, p. 73.
20. See Paul Lachance (tr. and ed.), *Angela of Foligno* (New York: Paulist Press, 1993).
21. Lachance, *Angela*, chap. 7, a, pp. 179–80.
22. Lachance, *Angela*, chap. 7, g, pp. 194–5.
23. Lachance, *Angela*, chap. 7, c, p. 182.
24. Lachance, *Angela*, chap. 8, c, p. 205.
25. Lachance, *Angela*, chap. 8, c, p. 205
26. Lachance, *Angela*, chap. 8, c, p. 206.
27. RCl 6:2.
28. 'The Blessed Angela of Foligno' in *The Essentials of Mysticism* (New York: E. P. Dutton & Co., 1920; Dutton paperback, 1960), pp. 160–82.
29. See Foreword in *Jacopone da Todi: The Lauds*, tr. Serge and Elizabeth Hughes (New York: Paulist Press, 1982), pp. xix–xxi.
30. Hughes and Hughes (tr.), *Jacopone da Todi*, p. 194.
31. Hughes and Hughes (tr.), *Jacopone da Todi*, p. 196.
32. An earlier version of these remarks on Scotus can be found in my study, *The Franciscans* (Collegeville MN: The Liturgical Press/ Michael Glazier Books, 1989), pp. 115–16.
33. *Opus Oxoniense*, III, d. 7, q. 3 (Vivès edn, XIV, 355a).
34. Cited by Allan Wolter, 'John Duns Scotus on the Primacy and Personality of Christ' in McElrath, *Franciscan Christology*, p. 141.
35. Frederick Faber, *The Blessed Sacrament* (Philadelphia: Reilly, 1958), p. 338, quoted in Gabriele Allegra, *My Conversations with Teilhard de Chardin on the Primacy of Christ: Peking 1942–1945*, tr. Bernardino M. Bonansea OFM (Chicago: Franciscan Herald Press, 1970), p. 94.
36. Cited by Wolter, in McElrath, *Franciscan Christology*, p. 153.
37. Emphasis added. *Opus Oxoniense*, III, d. 7, q. 3, n. 3 (Vivès edn, XIV, 355a), in Allegra, *Conversations*, p. 93.
38. *Opus Oxoniense* III, d. 20, q. unica, n. 10 (Vivès edn, XIV, 737b–738a), in Allegra, *Conversations*, p. 93 (my translation).
39. For a discussion of the texts, see Carolus Balic OFM, *Theologiae Marianae elementa* (Sibenik: Typographia Kačic, 1933).

3. 'The Poverty and Humility of Our Lord Jesus Christ'

1. SalVirt 2.
2. 1LAg 15–17.
3. See Duncan Nimmo, *Reform and Division in the Medieval Franciscan Order: From Saint Francis to the Foundation of the Capuchins* (*Bibliotheca Seraphico-Capuccina* 33) (Rome: Capuchin Historical Institute, 1987).
4. Test 16–17.
5. RegB 1:2.
6. Adm 14.
7. Adm 2.
8. Adm 4. The Earlier Rule contains a similar expression: 'Let no one appropriate to himself the charge of superior or the office of preacher' (RegnB 17).
9. Adm 7.
10. Adm 11.
11. Adm 14–15.
12. Adm 8.
13. Adm 1.
14. Adm 1.
15. RegB 6.
16. RegB 1.
17. Francis also uses a similar passage, from Luke 14:33, 'Whoever does not renounce everything cannot be my disciple', in Adm 3.
18. TestCl 13.
19. TestCl 19.
20. 4LAg 19–25.
21. RegCl 6:2.
22. Bartoli, *Clare*, p. 72.
23. Bartoli, *Clare*, p. 73.
24. LegCl 40, quoted in Bartoli, *Clare*, p. 188.
25. TestCl 10.
26. RegB 10:5–7.
27. Alberto Ghinato (ed.), *Chronicon seu Historia septem tribulationum ordinis minorum* (Rome: Antonianum, 1959).
28. Quoted in Nimmo, *Reform and Division*, pp. 95–6.
29. C. T. Davis (ed.) (Turin: Bottega di Erasmo, 1961), reproduction of the 1485 Venetian edition.
30. *Arbor vitae*, V, Cap. iii, col. 423; cf. *Mistici Francescani* II, pp. 663–4.

4. 'The Lord Led Me Among Them'

1. LaudDei 12; RegNb 23:28.
2. Test 1–3.
3. Fortini, *St Francis of Assisi*, chap. 6.

4. RegNb 9:3–6.
5. 2Cel. 98.
6. RegNb 8:12.
7. 'Lebbroso' in *Dizionario Francescano* (Padua: Messaggero, 1983), col. 851.
8. 1Cel 17.
9. 1Cel 103.
10. 2Cel 9.
11. LM 1:5.
12. LP 22.
13. LP 9.
14. *Chronicle of Jordan of Giano* 13, in Placid Herman OFM (ed. and tr.), *XIIIth Century Chronicles* (Chicago: Franciscan Herald Press, 1961).
15. Test 30.
16. *Chronicle* 33.
17. *Chronicle* 39.
18. *Memorial*, chap. V, in Lachance, *Angela*, pp. 162–3.
19. See *The Franciscans*, chap. 4, 'Brothers and Sisters of Penance', pp. 87–9.
20. John W. Diercksmeier (tr.) (New York: Crossroad, 1982); originally published as *Sâo Francisco de Assis: ternura e vigor. Uma leitura a partir dos pobres* (Colecâo Cefepal, 15) (Petrópolis RJ: Vozes/Cefepal, 1981).
21. See especially his third chapter, on Francis' contribution to the liberation of the oppressed.

5. 'The Spirit of Prayer and Holy Devotion'

1. RegB 5:3; 10:10.
2. EpAnt 2.
3. Adm 14.
4. RegB 3:1–5.
5. RegEr 7–9.
6. OffPass. Such devotional Offices were not uncommon in the Middle Ages.
7. LaudHor 10.
8. 2Cel 201.
9. EpOrd 38.
10. 2Cel 94–101.
11. LaudDei. The original parchment contains the autograph of Francis on one side, and on the other Leo's handwritten notes concerning this event. During this Lent Francis had a vision of a Seraph, to be discussed later.
12. RegB 3:6–8.
13. See 'Quaresima' in *Dizionario Francescano*, col. 1487–1500.
14. See Henrietta Leyser, *Hermits and the New Monasticism: A Study of*

Religious Communities in Western Europe 100–1150 (New York: St Martin's Press, 1984).

15. 1Cel 33.
16. 1Cel 36.
17. REr, title.
18. Thomas Merton, *Contemplation in a World of Action* (Garden City NY: Doubleday, 1971).
19. *Bonaventure*, p. 54.
20. *Bonaventure*, p. 111.
21. *Bonaventure*, pp. 112–33.
22. *Bonaventure*, p. 115.
23. Giovanni de Caulibus, *Meditationes Vitae Christi*, ed. Lázaro Iriarte, *Mistici Francescani* II, pp. 795–972. See Iriarte's comments on p. 801. The following translation is my own. An English version can also be found in Isa Ragusa, Rosalie B. Green (eds.), *Meditations on the Life of Christ* (Princeton: 1961).
24. *Meditationes* 104, cf. *Mistici Francescani* II, p. 971.
25. 'Herp' in *Dictionnaire de spiritualité*, col. 346. For a recent edition of the 'Mirror', in Latin and Spanish, see Juan Martín Kelly (tr. and ed.), *Directorio de contemplativos* (*Colección Espirituales Españoles, Serie B, Lecturas, t. 2*) (Madrid: Universidad Pontificia de Salamanca, Fundación Univ. Española, 1974).
26. *Directorium contemplativorum*, part 3, chap. 59, in Kelly (tr. and ed.), *Directorio de contemplativos*, p. 662.
27. Kieran Kavanaugh, 'Spanish Sixteenth Century: Carmel and Surrounding Movements' in *Christian Spirituality: High Middle Ages and Reformation*, p. 75 (see n. 2 of the Introduction to this book).
28. *Francisco de Osuna: The Third Spiritual Alphabet*, tr. Mary E. Giles (New York: Paulist Press, 1981).
29. *Misticos Franciscanos Españoles II* (*Biblioteca de Autores Cristianos*) (Madrid: Editorial Catolica, 1948), pp. 25–442.
30. *Ascent*, part 3, chap. 16, in *Misticos*, p. 370.
31. *Misticos*, p. 370.
32. *La Règle de perfection: The Rule of Perfection*, Jean Orcibal (ed.) (Paris: Presses universitaires de France, 1982).

6. 'By Your Holy Cross, You have Redeemed the World'

1. Test 6.
2. OffPass (Compline) 1:3.
3. For example, five 'Considerations' on the stigmata are appended at the end of the *Fioretti*.
4. See the comprehensive study of texts and art in Chiara Frugoni, *Francesco e l'invenzione delle stimmate* (Turin: Einaudi, 1993).
5. 1Cel 94.
6. 2Cel chaps. 135–8.

7. 1Cel 112.
8. 1Cel 36.
9. LM 13:10.
10. LM 13:5, translation from *Bonaventure*, p. 324.
11. *Memorial*, chap. III, in Lachance (ed.), *Angela*, p. 141.
12. Lachance (ed.), *Angela*, p. 85.
13. *Memorial*, chap. VI, in Lachance (ed.), *Angela*, pp. 175–6.
14. See Chiara Giovanna Cremaschi, 'Giacomo da Milano: Introduzione', *I mistici* I, pp. 801–4.
15. *Stimulus amoris*, chap. XIV (my translation); cf. *I mistici* I, pp. 848–9. Translated into English, with commentary, by Walter Hilton (d. 1396) as *The Goad of Love*. A modern English version can be found in C. Kirchberger, *The Goad of Love* (London: Faber and Faber, 1952).
16. See Carolyn Walker Bynum, *Jesus as Mother: Studies in the Spirituality of the High Middle Ages* (Berkeley: University of California Press, 1982).
17. *De Conformitate vitae beati Francisci ad vitam Domini Iesu* in *Analecta Franciscana* IV and V (Quaracchi: PP. Collegii S. Bonaventurae, 1906, 1912).
18. Cf. *I mistici*, pp. 1084–5.
19. Camilla Battista Varano, *Vita spirituale* in Giovanni Pozzi and Claudio Leonardi (eds.), *Scrittrici mistiche italiane* (Genoa: Marietti, 1988), p. 303.
20. *Vita spirituale* 8, in *Scrittrici*, p. 324.

7. 'Be Praised, My Lord, With All Your Creatures'

1. See the extensive studies by Edward Armstrong, *Saint Francis, Nature Mystic: The Derivation and Significance of the Nature Stories in the Franciscan Legend* (Berkeley: University of California Press, 1976); and Roger Sorrell, *St Francis of Assisi and Nature: Tradition and Innovation in Western Christian Attitudes toward the Environment* (New York: Oxford University Press, 1988).
2. 1Cel. 81.
3. 1Cel. 81.
4. Besides the translations in standard Franciscan collections, there are numerous English versions of this religious classic, e.g., Leo Shirley-Price (tr.), *The Little Flowers of Saint Francis With Five Considerations on the Sacred Stigmata* (Baltimore: Penguin Books, 1959).
5. Fior 22.
6. Fior 21.
7. See my earlier study, *Saints in the World of Nature: The Animal Story as Spiritual Parable in Medieval Hagiography A.D. 900–1200* (Rome: Pontifical Gregorian University, 1983).
8. For an earlier version of these remarks, see Short, *The Franciscans*, pp. 114–15.

9. 'The Life and Christological Thought of St. Bonaventure' in McElrath, *Franciscan Christology*, p. 63.

10. McElrath, *Franciscan Christology*, p. 79.

11. *The Soul's Journey* 2:11, in *Bonaventure*, pp. 75–6.

12. *Memorial*, chap. VI, in Lachance, *Angela*, pp. 169–70.

13. Commentary on Ecclesiastes, *Opera Omnia* (Quaracchi: Patres Collegii S. Bonaventurae, 1882–1902), VI, 16, quoted in Allegra, p. 81.

14. Allan Wolter (tr.), *A Treatise on God as First Principle* (Chicago: Franciscan Herald Press, 1966), p. 145.

15. *Opus Oxoniense* I, d. 2, q. 2, n. 31 (Vivès edn, VIII, 477), cited in Diomede Scaramuzzi OFM, *Duns Scoto, Summula: Scelta di scritti coordinati in dottrina* (Edizioni 'Testi Cristiani') (Florence: Libreria Editrice Fiorentina, 1932), p. 86.

16. *Ordinatio* I, d. 17, q. 1–2, n. 173 (Vatican edn, V, 222), cited in Gabriele Allegra, *My Conversations with Teilhard de Chardin on the Primacy of Christ: Peking 1942–1945*, tr. Bernardino M. Bonansea OFM (Chicago: Franciscan Herald Press, 1970), p. 89..

17. *Opus Oxoniense* Prol., q. 2, nn. 3–14 (Vivès edn, VIII, 77–10) in Scaramuzzi, *Duns Scoto*, p. 46.

18. *Der heilige Franziskus von Assisi. Ein Troubadour* (Strasbourg, 1826).

19. *Les Poètes franciscains en Italie au Treizieme siècle, avec un choix des Petites Fleurs de saint François traduites de l'italien* (Paris: 1852).

20. Journal 161, in Maurice B. McNamee SJ, 'Hopkins: Poet of Nature and of the Supernatural' in Norman Weyand SJ, *Immortal Diamond: Studies in Gerard Manley Hopkins* (New York: Sheed & Ward, 1949), p. 228.

21. Humphry House and Graham Storey (eds.), *The Journals and Papers of Gerard Manley Hopkins* (London: Oxford University Press, 1959), p. 408, quoted in J. Hillis Miller, 'The Univocal Chiming' in Geoffrey H. Hartman, *Hopkins: A Collection of Critical Essays* (Englewood Cliffs NJ: Prentice-Hall, 1966), p. 89.

22. Miller, *Chiming*, p. 111.

23. House, *Journals*, p. 254.

24. House, *Journals*, p. 207.

25. McNamee, 'Hopkins,' p. 231.

26. See *The Transcendentals and Their Function in the Metaphysics of Duns Scotus* (Washington: The Catholic University of America Press, 1946), pp. 31–57; see also Cyril L. Shircel OFM, *The Univocity of the Concept of Being in the Philosophy of John Duns Scotus* (Washington: Catholic University Press, 1942); and Etienne Gilson, *Jean Duns Scotus* (Paris: 1952).

27. Miller, *Chiming*, p. 113.

28. House, *Journals*, p. 199.

29. *Poems of Gerard Manley Hopkins*, ed. W. H. Gardner (New York: Oxford University Press, 3rd edn, 1949), p. 95.

30. *The Dragon in the Gate: Studies in the Poetry of G. M. Hopkins* (Berkeley and Los Angeles: University of California Press, 1968).

31. House, *Journals*, pp. 144–6, 364n, quoted in Schneider, *The Dragon in the Gate*, p. 116. In his study of 'The Dialectic of Sense-Perception' in *Hopkins*, Geoffrey H. Hartman gives another example from Hopkins' journals about this kind of close observation. He notes: 'Even when, as in a snowfall, it seems least possible to remark the individual forms of things, Hopkins still manages to do so':

> It tufted and toed the firs and yews and went to load them till they were taxed beyond their spring. The limes, elms, and Turkey-oaks it crisped beautifully as with young leaf. Looking at the elms from underneath you saw every wave in every twig ... and to the hangers and flying sprays it restored, to the eye, the inscapes they had lost. (Hartman, *Hopkins*, p. 123.)

32. Claude Colleer Abbott (ed.), *The Letters of Gerard Manley Hopkins to Robert Bridges* (London: Oxford University Press, 1955), III, p. 19, in Miller, *Chiming*, p. 111.

8. The Franciscan Tradition Today

1. My study of the history of the Franciscan family, *The Franciscans*.
2. I am indebted to my colleague Joseph Chinnici OFM for the phrase.

SELECTED BIBLIOGRAPHY

Franciscan Sources

Dizionario Francescano (Padua: Messaggero, 1983).

Fontes Franciscani, ed. Ernesto Menestò, Stefano Brufani et al. (S. Maria degli Angeli-Assisi: 1995).

Francis of Assisi: Early Documents (3 vols), ed. Regis J. Armstrong, J. A. Wayne Hellmann, William J. Short (New York: New City Press, 1999–).

Mistici Francescani, Secolo XIV, vol. II (Assisi: Editrici Francescane, 1997).

Scritti dei Mistici Francescani, Secolo XIII, I mistici, vol. I (Assisi: Editrici Francescane, 1995).

St Francis of Assisi, Writings and Early Biographies: English Omnibus of the Sources for the Life of St Francis, ed. Marion A. Habig (Chicago: Franciscan Herald Press, 1973).

Francis: Life and Writings

Fortini, Arnaldo, *Nova Vita di San Francesco* (Santa Maria degli Angeli, Italy: Tipografia Porziuncola, 1959); *Francis of Assisi*, tr. Helen Moak (New York: Crossroad, 1981).

Francis and Clare: The Complete Works, ed. Regis J. Armstrong and Ignatius Brady (Ramsey NJ: Paulist Press, 1982).

Manselli, Raoul, *San Francesco d'Assisi* (Rome: Bulzoni, 1980; 2nd, rev. edn, 1981). *St Francis of Assisi*, tr. Paul Duggan (Chicago: Franciscan Herald Press, 1988).

Clare: Life and Writings

Bartoli, Marco, *Chiara d'Assisi* (Rome: Istituto Storico dei Cappuccini, 1989); *Clare of Assisi*, tr. Sister Frances Teresa OSC (Quincy IL: Franciscan Press, 1993).

Carney OSF, Margaret, *The First Franciscan Woman: Clare of Assisi and Her Form of Life* (Quincy IL: Franciscan Press, 1993).

Clare of Assisi: Early Documents, ed. Regis J. Armstrong, (St Bonaventure NY: Franciscan Institute, 1990).

Peterson osf, Ingrid J., *Clare of Assisi: A Biographical Study* (Quincy IL: Franciscan Press, 1993).

Franciscan Authors

Angela of Foligno, *Angela of Foligno*, ed. Paul Lachance (New York: Paulist Press, 1993).

Angelo Clareno, *Chronicon seu Historia septem tribulationum ordinis minorum*, ed. Alberto Ghinato (Rome: Antonianum, 1959).

Bartholomew of Pisa, *De Conformitate vitae beati Francisci ad vitam Domini Iesu* in *Analecta Franciscana* IV and V (Quaracchi: PP. Collegii S. Bonaventurae, 1906, 1912).

Benet of Canfield, *La Règle de perfection: The Rule of Perfection*, ed. Jean Orcibal (Paris: Presses universitaires de France, 1982).

Bernardino de Laredo, *La Subida de Monte Sion* in *Misticos Franciscanos Españoles* II (*Biblioteca de Autores Cristianos*) (Madrid: Editorial Catolica, 1948), pp. 25–442.

Bonaventure of Bagnoregio, *The Soul's Journey into God* in *Bonaventure*, tr. Ewert Cousins (New York: Paulist Press, 1978).

Bonaventure of Bagnoregio, *What Manner of Man? Sermons on Christ by St. Bonaventure*, tr. Zachary Hayes ofm (Chicago: Franciscan Herald Press, 1974).

Francisco de Osuna, *The Third Spiritual Alphabet*, tr. Mary E. Giles (New York: Paulist Press, 1981).

Giovanni de Caulibus, *Meditationes Vitae Christi*, ed. Lázaro Iriarte, *Mistici Francescani* II, pp. 795–972; Isa Ragusa and Rosalie B. Green (eds.), *Meditations on the Life of Christ* (Princeton: 1961).

Herp, Hendrik, *Directorio de contemplativos* (*Colección Espirituales españoles, Serie B, Lecturas, t. 2*), tr. and ed. Juan Martín Kelly (Madrid: Universidad Pontificia de Salamanca, Fundación Univ. Española, 1974).

Jacopone da Todi, *Jacopone da Todi: The Lauds*, tr. Serge and Elizabeth Hughes (New York: Paulist Press, 1982).

James of Milan, *Stimulus amoris: The Goad of Love*, tr. C. Kirchberger (London: Faber and Faber, 1952).

Jordan of Giano, *Chronicle of Jordan of Giano* 13, in Placid Herman ofm (ed. and tr.), *XIIIth Century Chronicles* (Chicago: Franciscan Herald Press, 1961).

Ubertino da Casale, *Arbor vitae crucifixae Iesu*, ed. C. T. Davis (Turin: Bottega di Erasmo, 1961), reproduction of the 1485 Venetian edition.

Franciscan History, Spirituality

Armstrong, Edward, *Saint Francis, Nature Mystic: The Derivation and Significance of the Nature Stories in the Franciscan Legend* (Berkeley: University of California Press, 1976).

Boff, Leonardo, *São Francisco de Assis: ternura e vigor. Uma leitura a partir dos pobres* (Colecâo Cefepal, 15) (Petrópolis RJ: Vozes/Cefepal, 1981); *Saint Francis: A Model for Human Liberation*, tr. John W. Diercksmeier (New York: Crossroad, 1982).

'Frères Mineurs' ('Spiritualité franciscaine') in *Dictionnaire de Spiritualité, Ascetique et Mystique* (Paris: Beauchesne, 1962) V, col. 1268–1422.

Frugoni, Chiara, *Francesco e l'invenzione delle stimmate* (Turin: Einaudi, 1993).

Lekeux OFM, Martial, *Franciscan Mysticism*, tr. Dom Basil Whelman OSB (London: Sheed and Ward, 1928; Pulaski, Wisconsin: Franciscan Publishers, repr. 1956).

Lekeux OFM, Martial, *Short-Cut to Divine Love*, tr. Paul J. Oligny OFM (Chicago: Franciscan Herald Press, 1962).

McElrath, Damian (ed.), *Franciscan Christology* (St Bonaventure NY: Franciscan Institute Publications, 1980).

Merton, Thomas, 'Franciscan Eremitism' in *Contemplation in a World of Action* (Garden City NY: Doubleday, 1971).

Nimmo, Duncan, *Reform and Division in the Medieval Franciscan Order: From Saint Francis to the Foundation of the Capuchins (Bibliotheca Seraphico-Capuccina* 33) (Rome: Capuchin Historical Institute, 1987).

Short, William, *The Franciscans* (Collegeville MN: The Liturgical Press/ Michael Glazier Books: 1989).

Sorrell, Roger, *St. Francis of Assisi and Nature: Tradition and Innovation in Western Christian Attitudes toward the Environment* (New York: Oxford University Press, 1988).